MW00566003

Pray Your Way to Happiness

Rev. Robert DeGrandis, S.S.J.

Acknowledgement

A special "thank you" is extended to Gene Koshenina of Clear Lake, Texas, for his additions to this book.

Copyright © 1999 by Robert DeGtrandis,S.S.J.

Printed in the United Sstates of America

ISBN 1-893403-00-9

Table of Contents

Introduction

As Christians, we continually hear the words of Jesus proclaimed: "You shall love the Lord your God with all your heart, with all your soul, and with all your mind, and with all your strength" (Mark 12:30, NAB).

We have heard this so often that it has failed to have the impact it should. In the early days of the Church, men and women went into the desert to live out this command. That was the beginning of monasticism, which is still strong today. However, Jesus knows that most of us will have to live that out in life as a lay person, and he expects us to be faithful each day as we try to live this proclamation.

Prayer is a subject people want to hear about. Few are offended when you bring up this subject in a gathering. Most have an instinctive desire to speak to God, but often they feel incapable or unworthy. We want to encourage people to begin or to continue this noble endeavor.

We should be spending some time each day communicating with the Lord Jesus, asking His strength and inspiration to be conscientious Christians living His Word. That is why Prayer is so important. He will guide and direct us to walk in His holy will.

Prayer is being utilized in secular life today. A medical doctor who prescribes prayer for the patients said they generally accept it well. They appreciate the love and concern. However, there was one exception. "I never met a doctor like you," she said, "Give me my medicine." So, she did receive it, but also an exhortation to pray for the health of her soul.

More and more we read about spiritual subjects such as prayer in the daily paper or see television programs dealing with the spiritual. The media is responding to the criticism that they are missing the best stories today about people's spiritual journeys. We will read more about spiritual subjects in the future, and prayer will be one of the topics. There will be increased demand for more materials on spirituality, especially prayer. This book can be a help to some.

A magazine ran an article on prayer and many people responded with surprising answers. Questioned about their time of prayer, 8% said they prayed one minute or less, 47% said five minutes or less, and 28% indicated they prayed an hour or more. It is astonishing that an article on prayer would appear in a secular magazine, but more importantly, that so many would assert that they prayed as much as they said they did.

I recently saw some "atheistic" bumper stickers on the back of a pickup truck which attacked religion. One of them caught my eye. It read: "Prayer Always Fails." It has been reported that there are over 3,000 registered atheists in the State of Texas. However, to encounter one like this was a shock. It does make people take a stand. Do you believe in prayer or not? Many lukewarm Christians will be forced to take sides, and this may help them come back to the Lord. They will be shocked as I was. We will be seeing more situations like this in the future as people become more pagan.

I read the following article about a group of doctors in the Pittsburgh, Pennsylvania area recently. It mentions that professionals are now praying with their patients:

PITTSBURGH (AP) – "A trip to the doctor typically ends with a prescription, a pat on the back and a bill. Three idealists in one of the city's poorest neighborhoods have added God to the mix.

"The doctors at the new North Side Christian Health Center ask patients to pray with them at the end of each appointment.

" 'I've not had anyone refuse,' said Dr. Daniel Holt, who abandoned dreams of being a pastor, to treat the poor. 'One

6

woman reached out and gave me a hug when we were done.'

"The doctors who do not discriminate by religion, say an experimental arrangement with a hospital lets them minister as they heal -- a longtime dream of each. Since the clinic opened in January, Drs. Holt, Todd Wahrenberger and Mark Guy have spent a day or two a week there. The rest of the week, they treat residents of the middle-class suburb of West View. In effect, the doctors have surrendered one-third of their earning power.

"The North Side clinic does not make money. One-third of the 54,000 people in the neighborhood are poor under the federal governmental definition. Half of the patients seen in the clinic's first three months had no health insurance. People pay only what they can afford -- sometimes nothing."[1]

In the 70's, six of my books were published in Brazil. Today, none of those books are available except "THE TEN COMMANDMENTS OF PRAYER"[2], which has gone through fourteen printings. That would indicate that there is almost always a deep interest in prayer even when other subjects of religious nature lose their appeal.

By incorporating prayer into your daily life, may you have new eyes to see your life, your family and your community with God's eyes. "Have among yourselves the same attitude that is also yours in Christ Jesus " (Philippians 2:5, NAB).

The principles and suggestions in this booklet can be a great help to building a strong prayer life, binding you to Jesus and assisting you to love the Lord with your whole heart. Meditate and reflect upon each rule. It can help you to understand the incredible power of prayer. Many of us have seen miracles flow from prayer in our own lives and those of our family members. Consider each suggestion carefully.

Lord Jesus, give each person who reads this book a new gift of prayer, that they may give themselves more fully to praise and honor Our Heavenly Father, and may their family receive many blessings and healings.

Amen.

Chapter I

Pray As You Can, Not As You Can't

"Ask and it will be given to you; seek and you will find, knock and the door will be opened to you" (Matthew 7:7, NAB).

The human heart feels a desire to be in union with a higher power that can give it strength, life, happiness, and health. God placed that desire and urge in every heart so that we would be drawn to Him in prayer and love. We want to become more intimate with God, and so we want to please Him. We also have needs that we feel inept at fulfilling, and thus we ask God to help us. As Christians, we should see Jesus in every person, and thus we want to love and help them. We should feel happy when others have success and are joyful, and sad when they are hurt in some way.

When we pray, we are giving ourselves to God. He sees our intention and that is sufficient. A little child may pick a prize rose from the garden for the mother, and she is horrified. However, she understands the love of the little one and she accepts the "thoughtfulness" of the child. So Our Heavenly Father understands our desire to communicate with Him, and He accepts that. It is our good will that He is looking for. We want to give Him our love, and that touches His Heart. We may not do very well in our prayer, and we may even fall asleep during the whole prayer time. But God eagerly accepts our love.

> "*Prayer is a vital necessity*...**Nothing is equal to prayer; for what is impossible it makes possible, what is difficult, easy....For it is impossible, utterly impossible, for the man who prays eagerly and invokes God ceaselessly ever to sin (St. John Chrysostrom, *De Anna*).**"

(The Catholic Catechism, # 2744)[3]

Prayer is generally defined as "communication that is pleasing to God". Prayer is attempted raising of the heart and mind to God, a desire to be in union with Him. Prayer is work done in obedience to or in honor of God. Prayer is primarily a matter of the heart, a desire to communicate with God. The very desire to pray is itself a prayer, as it is an attempt to be in union with God. "**Thus, the life of prayer is the habit of being in the presence of the thrice-holy God and in communion within**" (Catechism #2565).[4]

Prayer is obviously an act of love of God. A very holy man who was afflicted with a brain tumor could only make noises and look at the crucifix. That was "powerful prayer". With his heart he was attempting to communicate with the Lord. The Lord saw his heart. If I wink at a person, that communicates. There are no words, but if one reaches out to tenderly hold a person's hand, that is communication. Dancing for the Lord can also be a form of communication and prayer, even though it may be "non-verbal'. It can be an expression of joy in the Lord.

We usually think of prayer as vocal or mental sentences or thoughts to or about God or His "things". But prayer can be our work, **prayer on the job**, offered up to God. We accomplish this by offering to God all of our sacrifices and, don't forget, part of our rewards too. Many people support a family, and this becomes prayer when we offer it to God. Tithing towards the house and servants of the Lord and other charitable causes such as helping financially poor people is the usual method of returning a portion back to God. Of course, any act of love towards God or someone else is a prayer; it is sometimes clothed in a different form.

One excellent way to view our world is to think of it as a stage where we are performing before God, Mary, and all of the angels and saints. We are also performing before Lucifer and his hierarchy of devils. On this stage our actions are viewed by all, daily. One important question that arises is, who is our supporting cast at various times during the day, God and His entourage, or Lucifer and his. It depends on our thoughts, our actions, our intentions. God, of course, turns a deaf ear to

11

the ungodly; that is Satan's realm. There is never a question as to whom we communicate with when we pray to God and His own, it is always God!

For whom should we pray? We should pray for all people, but the closer they are to us, the more time we should spend praying for them; we should pray especially for ourselves. We should also pray for unbelievers, the souls in Purgatory, and the sick and suffering of the world because they are in great need of our prayers. We receive great blessings when we pray for our enemies. We need not pray for saints or angels, because they have no need for prayer. We cannot pray for demons and expect them to benefit because, while God loves them, they hate God with a growing, undying hatred and are thus beyond our ability to help. Rather, we should pray to St. Michael the Archangel to strengthen our cause against them.

Is there a best place to pray? Of course, in front of the Blessed Sacrament, but usually that is not possible. So the best answer may be, **we can and should pray everywhere**. In particular, we should pray in those places that help us pray more easily and whole-heartedly such as churches and shrines, but we need to feel comfortable talking to God at home and at work where we spend most of our time. One suggestion is that we create our own little prayer area at home such as a table or dresser upon which we place crucifixes, holy water, and pictures of Jesus, Mary, Joseph, of archangels Michael, Gabriel, and Raphael, of angels, saints and others. Another suggestion is, if we are able, to make pilgrimages to Fatima, Lourdes, Guadalaupe, and Medjugorje. The blessings we receive far exceed our sacrifices.

How did Jesus pray? The Catholic Catechism[5] reads:

> **"There is strong evidence that Jesus always began His prayer with thanksgiving. For example, Jesus confesses the Father, acknowledges and blesses Him because He has hidden the mysteries of the Kingdom from those who think themselves learned and has revealed them to infants, the poor of the beatitudes (Matthew 11:22 NAB)"** (#2603)."

On one occasion, before the raising of Lazarus, Jesus said "…Father, I thank you for hearing me. I know that you always hear me…" (John 11:41-42, NAB). Of course, Jesus most renowned prayer is in the bible, the "Our Father". Perhaps Mary's most renouned prayers are the Rosary and the Canticle of Mary, the Magnificat (Latin).

According to Catechism of the Catholic Church[6]

> **"Jesus' prayer is the perfect model of prayer in the New Testament. Often done in solitude, the prayer of Jesus involves a loving adherence to the will of the Father, even to the Cross, and an absolute confidence in being heard "** (#2620).

There is a tendency to compare our prayer with that of others. Each of us is unique. God may lead you in one way, and lead your brother or sister in another way. In this time when many feel called to recite the rosary, a large segment prefers to read the scriptures. Prayer is like shoes. You choose the pair that fits and feels good for you. No one else can tell you what is satisfying to you. We are all different, and our personalities and temperaments vary, so each has to find the proper way to communicate with the Lord. Some enjoy:

Reading prayers

Singing or playing spiritual songs

Dancing before the Lord

Praying spontaneously

Listening to music in prayful meditation

Sitting and adoring the Blessed Sacrament

Basking in Jesus' Presence

Prostrating oneself before the Tabernacle

Gazing at a statue or picture, and talking to Jesus

Writing their prayers in a journal

Praying together with another person

Reciting the rosary and meditating on its mysteries

Saying the Stations of the Cross

Reflecting on Holy Scripture or a spiritual book

Praying Novenas

What posture should we assume when we are praying? Most people kneel. But Charismatics often stand and pray with hands uplifted, which is quite scriptural. "It is my wish, then, that in every place the men should pray, **lifting up holy hands, without anger or argument..." (1Timothy 2:8,NAB).** Yet, if one were to do this on Sunday in some Catholic Churches, a few people would be offended. **Let each person be free to pray the way that fits him or her best.**

The following story illustrates how we can even be lying on our face and pray effectively. A drowning man does not use long repetitive prayers when he is calling out to the Lord. A wonderful prayer is, "Help, help!"

Downed pilot credits God's love, Marines' heroics for his rescue

WASHINGTON (CNS) – "While everyone was hailing him as a hero, Capt. Scott F. O'Grady, the downed Air Force pilot who was rescued June 8 from northern Bosnia, credited his faith, his training and heroic Marines for bringing him home.

" 'The first thing I want to do is thank God. If it wasn't for God's love for me and my love for God I wouldn't be here,' he said at a press conference held at an air base in Aviano, Italy, two days after his dramatic rescue.

" 'He's the one who delivered me. I

know it in my heart,' added the 29 year-old O'Grady.

" 'When I was out there, I heard all your prayers, heard them loud and clear,' he told a cheering crowd June 11 at Andrews Air Force Base in Maryland, just outside Washington.

"He was greeted there by his father, William O'Grady of Alexandria, Va., and his mother, Mary Lou Scardapane, who lives in Seattle, where she is a member of St. Benedict Catholic Church. Also on hand were his brother and sister, Paul and Stacy, his grandmother and grandfather and several hundred onlookers.

"For the six days O'Grady was in the Bosnian forest after his F-16 was shot down June 2, he survived on ants, grass and rainwater. He said he avoided capture by Serbian soldiers patrolling within a few yards of his hiding place by lying face down in the bushes, his camouflage helping him blend in with the vegetation. (Maureen Leonard)[7]

There are some who pray while lying in bed. That is the best position for them, and the Lord accepts whatever they feel comfortable with. Some of my friends prostrate themselves when they are alone; or they kneel before the Tabernacle. This is what speaks to their hearts. Be yourself in your relationship with the Lord. In this respect God is like a shoe salesman who puts out many pairs of shoes and then says, "Take what fits you." Africans frequently pray quite differently than Americans. Drums are usual in Africa, but not in America. Whatever suits people most is the way they should go to God. Each person has to find his or her own way.

St. Therese of Lisieux said that when she slept in prayer she felt she was on her Father's lap, so that time was passed with Him and it was very profitable. There are no losers in the prayer ministry. When our intentions are to please God in prayer, we *are* pleasing Him. It is wonderful to have good feelings and high spiritual fulfillment in prayer. Sometimes we will have these experiences, but not always. We need to thank the Lord for these extraordinary experiences.

A group of men were talking about their prayer life and how they liked to pray. They were recounting the best prayer times they had. One man who worked for the electric company said: "The best prayer time I have ever had with the Lord was when I was dangling by one leg from the pole upside down calling on Jesus to save me. I really prayed!"

Contemplative people often move into action when the Holy Spirit leads them. Because of their prayer life, they have great motivation. We can look into the life of Mother Theresa and see proof of this. She moved through the streets of Calcutta ministering to the poor, the sick and dying, the people ignored and uncared for in her land.

The most frequently overlooked prayer is *suf-*

fering offered up to God. This is a powerful prayer. When we suffer, we can participate with Christ in His passion by offering it up. A form of suffering is self-denial, and we can all do this in some way. We can fast two days a week consuming only bread and water, we can cut down on television, we can dedicate less time to sports and the newspaper, and we can spend less time and money shopping for non-essentials. When the apostles informed Jesus they were unable to cure some people, Jesus told them that for some severe cases much prayer and fasting was necessary. Praying in groups is also very powerful. Thus, you are encouraged to belong to a prayer group.

What is comfortable for you? Follow that way! Thank the Lord for the beauties of nature. This happens to many men who go hunting and fishing, they have a spiritual experience with nature. The beauty of creation often awakens in us an experience of the Creator. Many Catholics believe you can only pray in silence, while others quote "worship the Lord with cries of gladness" (Psalm 100:2, NAB). I think it helps to be able to pray both ways so one has greater variety.

At the wailing wall in Jerusalem, I was intrigued by the Jewish men rocking back and forth reciting the psalms. It was evident that these men in motion were most serious about their communication with God. That was beautiful prayer because it involved the whole person, but I am not attracted by that style of prayer. That is for "admiration" by me, but not "imitation".

The greatest obstacle to prayer by far is mortal sin, but any sin erodes our will to pray, and results in the lack of love and desire to pray. The second greatest obstacle is unforgiveness of ourselves and others. The remedy is obvious. We should receive the Sacrament of Reconciliation once a month, or more often if possible. The power of this sacrament to reunite us to God and to increase our intimacy with Him is awesome. Our archenemy, Satan, is especially eager to place obstacles in our path to reconciliation, knowing that in a weakened state we are less prone to prayer and far more prone to sin.

Another powerful obstacle to prayer is discouragement. Discouragement often results from distractions. Mental distractions to prayer are everyday problems and excitements, dryness, doubt, a feeling of hopelessness, and fatigue. Virtually everything in the world can be an obstacle to prayer, but experience has shown me that our everyday business problems are one of the greatest obstacles, in addition to strong guilt feelings. Reciting three Rosaries daily, in which we ask for an increase of Faith and Hope, and praying the "Our Father" fifteen times will greatly alleviate these problems.

Fatigue is a common but rather poor excuse for not praying, because Our Lord was exhausted on His way to the cross, yet He prayed to Our Father even as he was dying on the cross. The following prayer to God Our Father was recited earlier in the Garden of Gethsemane by a very tired, dejected Jesus: " Then He said to them, 'My soul is sorrowful even to death. Remain here and keep watch with me.' He advanced a little and fell prostrate in prayer saying, 'My Father, if it is possible, let this cup pass from me; yet not as I will, but as you will' " (Matthew 26:38-39, NAB).

There are times when we will be dry, and will want to do anything but communicate with the Lord. Some saints have said that these are the *best* times for prayer because it takes more love to spend time with the Lord. There was one priest who tied himself physically to the kneeler when he experienced dryness. The Lord gives us the option of quietly walking around the chapel or room, and this can help. We must experience dryness, this purification from time to time so that we are praying for God's glory and not just for our good feelings.

Dryness in prayer is usually a sign that we are growing up spiritually, as long as we are trying to lead a good life. Sometimes dryness in prayer is a vital step in spiritual growth. It is important to know that the Lord is purposely taking away emotions and consolations to bring us up to a higher state of spiritual maturity. A good spiritual director recognizes God at work in the soul. We give lollipops to little children, but as adults we do not need them. The Lord has taken the lollipop of good feelings away, and now we are doing the mature work of a Christian, often without feelings.

St. Francis de Sales draws an image of a deaf violinist playing for the King. Although the musician could not hear a thing, he knew that the King was pleased with the music. In the same way, Our Father is happy with our prayer even though it is dry, and we ourselves get no emotional kick. This is difficult for most people because in the beginning we generally tend to get a good feeling out of prayer. As we mature, it becomes more an act of the will rather than a *feeling* experience.

God desires our heart. He wants us to give ourselves to Him totally, not just when it feels good. We choose Him over our feelings. We pray to give God glory, not to feel good. Consider the sufferings of the martyrs. They no doubt were praying as they were being slaughtered. In their pain, they knew that God heard their petitions, and that was sufficient for them. Most of us have experienced crying out to Our Father in the midst of pain, knowing He was attentive to our prayer.

Someone has said that "There is work that is done on the mountaintop that cannot be done in the valleys, and there is work done in us by God in the valleys that cannot be done on the mountaintop". We sometimes have great experiences in prayer, and we receive great healing. It is sometimes very painful as we try to pray for that great healing. God is always in charge, and he sees our prayer and blesses us.

One time I was viewing a video of a mystic who was suffering the wounds of Jesus on Good Friday. The woman was writhing in pain as she experienced the pains of her Lord. She was continually in prayer, but there was nothing evident but pain. Her prayer was most powerful even

21

though the torment was excruciating. Admittedly this was a unique situation, but it points to prayer being most fruitful as a matter of will, not necessarily emotions.

At funerals, we pray without positive emotions. We are sad and depressed at the loss of a relative or friend, but we pray deeply for their soul. Grieving can be very painful, but we are able to communicate with God powerfully, with deep intensity. Frequently, we cry out to God in pain. Many people come back to a relationship with their Heavenly Father at this difficult time, truly understanding the fragility and shortness of life. We ourselves know how deeply we pray at this time. It is one of the most teachable moments in our life. Most of us have experienced not wanting to go to Church on Sunday because we did not feel good or were not in the mood. We forced ourselves to attend Holy Mass and to give glory to God. That is excellent prayer! We made the choice to worship God. We put Him first, and ourselves second. That is the Christian way.

G. K. Chesterton, the famous English philosopher and author, said: "It is difficult to live as a Catholic, but it is easy to die as a Catholic." The following verses capture that same idea, and that is why Jesus said, "Whoever does not take up his cross and follow after me is not worthy of me" (Matthew 10:38, NAB):

CHRISTIANITY
In the home it is kindness.
In the business it is honesty.

In society it is courtesy.
In work it is fairness.
Toward the unfortunate it is empathy.
Toward the weak it is help.
Toward the wicked it is resistance.
Toward the strong it is trust.
Toward the penitent it is forgiveness.
Toward the successful it is congratulations.
And towards God it is reverence and obe-
dience.[8]

Prayer is a matter of will and not necessarily of emotions. Teresa J. Cleary, of Cincinnati, Ohio, cried out to God in her frustration.

"As I raced from post office to hardware store to office-supply warehouse, the whines from my three tired and hungry kids rose to an ear-splitting level. With only half my errands accomplished, I was just as crabby as they were. At the stoplight, I rested my head on the wheel. "Lord, I'm frustrated. What am I supposed to do?" A beep from the driver behind me told me the light had changed. As I raised my head, my eyes focused on the license plate of the car ahead of me. In bold blue letters was my reply: BJOYFUL."[9]

What a wonderful answer to prayer! This woman was lifted up by what some would say was coincidence, but she knew it was a response from God.

Lord, help me find the ways I can pray best and thus enter into union with you in a more complete manner. Also, give me a desire to try new ways that may open new doors for me. Let me feel the joy of giving you time each day, even when I don't feel like praying. There are many duties I have to perform, but let me understand the value of giving back some of the time you give me.

Amen

Chapter II

Pray As A Little Child

"Amen, I say to you, whoever does not accept the kingdom of God like a child will not enter it" (Mark 10:15, NAB).

**"...He who humbles himself will be exalted*; humility is the foundation of prayer"* (Catechism #2559)[10].

God is humble, and He calls us to be simple and sincere in our relationship with Him. Just consider how a little child will crawl up on the parent's lap and simply rest there. Often the child will come and simply ask for this or that, like bread and jam. The parent is so happy to be able to give something good to the child. Some parents just cannot do enough for their children. They "live" for their children. They may spoil them too much, but it gives parents such joy to see their children happy.

"Jesus says: 'If you then, who are wicked know how to give good things to your children, how much more will your heavenly Father give good things to those who ask'" (Matthew 7:11, NAB).

With children there are some avenues of love that one must take for the child's development. TIME WITH, is so important. Children need the parent to give them quality time to model proper behavior and to share love. TALK WITH means communicating when they want to appropriately talk. TENDERNESS is a must. They must feel love so that they can feel valuable and lovable. TRUST is another ingredient of a healthy upbringing.

These qualities are also necessary in our prayer life. We must spend TIME WITH the Lord Jesus, ideally, an hour a day. To TALK WITH Jesus means being like that little child with a parent, a friend, a brother. There will be TENDERNESS as we feel His Love and Presence from time to time, and this will give rise to tenderness in our heart. Finally, TRUST will develop so that all of our wants, needs, and desires will be put into His Hands. Read the following letter I received:

"It was the saddest time of my life and I was desperately in need of God, but I could not pray. My sixteen year old son had committed suicide and I felt like my life was over, too, and even though I went through the motions of living, I felt dead inside. No hope. No joy -- just existing and trying to get through each day.

"I would open the Bible - but couldn't read. I would start a prayer -- but couldn't finish. Parts of Bible verses came to mind, occasionally, but the only prayer that stayed with me was "Jesus." That's as long as my concentration span was, and I said this WORD over and over again! Sometimes in anger, sometimes in agony, sometimes in frustration, or sorrow or guilt or questioning.

"And Jesus, who could see into my heart, listened to it all, and slowly but surely He healed me and continues to heal me as I put my trust in Him.

"I no longer feel hopeless and joyless, and I know now that my Lord never did abandon me. All I had to do was say His name!"

Thank you Jesus!

D.P.

Aberdeen, SD

We must be humble as a little child when we pray. Jesus is God, yet He so *humbly* chose to come into the world as a helpless infant. He had to be clothed and fed. Born and placed in a manger that supplied food to animals, Jesus was destined to become the food for our sanctification in the Eucharist. Born an *apparently* ordinary baby, Jesus was the ruler over all of creation, and the judge of all beings. Jesus' coming into the world was so humble, virtually unheralded other than by scripture. Only three wise men, who were Gentiles, and some Jewish shepherds were directly apprised of the greatest event since the creation of the world. Jesus was taught to pray by Mary, and He Himself humbly prayed with Mary as a little child.

"Those who want to fully participate in the ministry of Jesus Christ *must* become humble." Otherwise, Jesus probably can't give you as much work as he would like to because you aren't capable of doing much, nor of doing it well. How can you measure your humility? One way is by the company "you choose" to keep. If you abide only with high achievers, the successful, those of affluence, chances are that you are not very humble. But if you graciously talk to those considered uneducated, unintelligent, or unskilled chances are good that you are "meek and humble of heart" and close to God. Another powerful sign that you have achieved humility is by your degree of forgiveness. You may have many enemies, but you must not have any that you do not forgive "with the help of Jesus". The key is to have Jesus help you. It is folly to think you can forgive by yourself. Just wait until the right circumstances present themselves and watch that anger rise, and sometimes overflow out of control. As you pray the "Our Father" you can say, "and forgive us our trespasses, as **we forgive** those who trespass against us (**with Jesus' help**); and lead us not…

28

"We must all become more humble." This is essential, because humility is the foundation of the cross. Humility supports forgiveness. And Faith is the upright post of the cross, which raises Hope and Charity to new and greater heights. Through frequent worthy reception of the blessed sacraments, especially in daily Holy Eucharist, we increase humility and Faith most surely and steadily. Another wonderful way to greater Faith is to praise God intensively for 20 minutes every day, praying in tongues, the language of the Holy Spirit. In doing this we emulate Mary, the Virgin Mother. Did she not solely have the great faith that Jesus would rise from the dead in three days!

Clearly, God always gave the most important work to the humblest people that were on earth at the time. Abraham, Moses, and Mary are good examples as well as Joseph, and St. John the Baptist. Of course, Jesus infinitely surpassed them in every respect as the man-God who held all power in heaven and on earth. With but a thought and an affirmative "I want it", He could do ANYTHING! Yet in His great humility, Jesus even allowed Himself to be under the power of the devil bodily while fasting in the desert, and later under the power of Lucifer and Judas and Pontius Pilate in the same manner during His passion and death. He suffered this for our sake so that we could be redeemed, made co-heirs of heaven with Him.

Is there a most powerful prayer? **Clearly, the Eucharist worthily received is our greatest prayer**, and nothing can compare with it and nothing can substitute for it. Only the Catholic Church has the real presence of Jesus in the Eucharist. Even children can receive the Eucharist. How wise we too are, like the three wise men, when we visit the household of Jesus and partake of His living presence in the most blessed sacrament of the "Holy Eucharist". We should be ecstatic to receive this incomprehensible sacrament even once in our lifetime, but Jesus allows us to receive Him daily. We need not prepare for years or months for this greatest event. We were freed from that, from rigorous rules and regulations, by Our Lord.

We have all heard of parents who have gone into debt or taken another job to be able to provide health care or education for their children. Just as parents will go out of their way to please their children, so our Heavenly Father wants to bless us more than we can know or desire. He will bring people and events into our lives that will be a real blessing. We try to do the very best for our children. How much more, then, does our Heavenly Father want to do the very best for us, to bless us. Consider the following testimony:

What Prayer Can Do

"At the age of 36 I decided to return to college. As I signed the registration forms in the bursar's office the cashier said, 'The charge is five hundred and nineteen dollars. If you do not have the money now, you can pay next week when you start your first class'.

"I didn't have the money then. In fact, I wasn't sure I'd have it the next week either, but my desire to complete my education was strong. 'Dear Lord,' I prayed as I left the office, "if you want me to do this, help me to find a way.

"In the late afternoon I stopped at the Department of Motor Vehicles to renew my driver's license. After scanning my forms the clerk asked me about a name transfer I had made several years earlier on my car. Then she excused herself to confer with a supervisor. What now? I fretted, 'Give it to her,' I heard the supervisor say.

"When the clerk returned, she was smiling. 'We owe you some money on that transfer a few years back,' she said. 'We're going to give it to you now. It comes to five hundred and forty dollars.'

"God had not only answered my prayer for the means to continue my education; He added a little bonus too! (Margaret Walsh, West Hills, California)[11]

As we become even more tender and loving children of our Heavenly Father, we can go to him just as to an earthly father, and get the help we need to get through the problems. I often went to my earthly father for help. There was nothing that my father could not fix. He had wise advice whenever I presented a problem. Often I would ask him for some coins to go to the store for candy, and he would say: "You cannot have everything you want in life, so you have to learn to do without." That was all right with me, as I saw his wisdom. Today, I thank him for that training. In our materialistic society we are bombarded with advertisements. I have financial discipline; I learned to do without many unnecessary "conveniences".

The following testimony shows the wisdom flowing from the Father in this very practical situation which many of us endure:

Words That Change People

"Everyone has some source of irritation that seems chronic. Several years ago, mine was taxi drivers. I felt I was forever being overcharged by Washington, D.C. cab drivers, who have no meters to register fares.

"Settling back in a cab one day, I suddenly remembered something Dr. Emmet Fox, the famous author and clergyman, had said: 'If a problem bothers you, try blessing it.' And so, silently I blessed the driver, thinking all the while that he would gyp me, which he proceeded to do. It didn't occur to me until later that my negative thoughts might have canceled my rather hesitant blessing.

"But one evening, when traffic was heavy and I stood on the street signaling, three men moved into a better spot ahead of me. Instead of blowing my top as I usually did in such situations, I blessed them. Around the corner came a cab. It passed the three men and pulled up for me. 'How did you happen to stop by me?' I asked as I got in.

"The driver grinned. 'Perhaps the good Lord just intended it!'

Coincidence? Maybe. But try blessing it. Those words changed my whole approach to life. From that day on, I learned that by blessing people - especially those who wrong me -- my life can be ruled by understanding, not by anger" (J.N. (Bill) Bailey, June 1959).[12]

Those who wish to develop a stronger relationship with the Father may find the "Our Father" prayer most helpful. Many have reported to me how praying the Rosary brings peace to them, great harmony into their lives. Some have told me how the Psalms have helped increase their love of God, and others have stated that the Magnificat helps them with "praise". Prayers orientated towards the passion and death of Our Savior are especially pleasing to the Father. For example, we can offer to Our Father, for His great pleasure, "The Way of the Cross", or we can reflect on the image of the disfigured face of "Jesus Crucified" on the Shroud of Turin. We can pray "The Chaplet of Mercy". We should pray the way we are the most inclined, the way we most "feel like praying".

The *most perfect prayer* ever composed is the

"Our Father". This is hardly a surprise, since Jesus, the Man-God, was the one who created it and passed it along to His Disciples. Intensely prayed, it will heal us in all ways, physically, intellectually, emotionally, spiritually, and relationally. We should say this prayer through three Rosaries daily, according to the children of Medjugorje.

"Our Father, Who art in heaven, hallowed be Thy name." God is present in a special way in heaven, the Father, Son, and Holy Spirit, thus He is three times holy. "Thy kingdom come, thy will be done, on earth as it is in heaven." And so, Father, I want your law to be the law of the land, your will to be obeyed so that there is harmony and peace on earth as in heaven. "Give us this day our daily bread." Dear Father, help me grow in holiness, grant me precious pearls from the treasure house built by Jesus' passion and death. "And forgive us our sins, as we forgive those who sin against us (with Jesus help)"; Father, I know you will prevent (and heal) mental and physical illness, cancer and heart disease, as long as I recite this faithfully. "And lead us not into temptation." Father, I am not proud, and I know I can fall, put me not to the test. "But deliver us from evil." Protect me from the evil one, and from my own more or less good or evil heart.

"Amen". So be it, my Dearest Father, I want it!

We should make time to talk to God as a familiar friend, in private prayer. We always seem to have or make time to talk to people we really "want" to, and to do those things we really want to do. We can't honestly say we don't have time to pray, because we can pray short prayers many times each day. Also, we need to begin and end each day with a prayer. That is the recommendation of Our Lady as expressed to the children of Medjugorje. Mary said that when we begin and end the day with prayer, the whole day is a prayer. This means that all of the work we do for a living can become a prayer if we offer it to God. Surely we can pray morning and evening and during the day at appropriate times, what an easy thing to do for so great a benefit.

We need to pray as frequently as we can during the day to gain strength and power for living a holy, happy, more healed life. When we are working we occasionally take a break. We can include a loving thought of God at this time, or say a short prayer. If we are watching television, we can pray during commercials. We have many opportunities to pray, if we really think about it. Most of us travel to work and we could pray at that time, even when driving an automobile. If we properly prioritize, most of us should be able to find an hour a day to pray. Our Creator would never leave us for long in a situation in which we couldn't find sufficient time to pray.

We can and should rise to a higher level of prayer through meditation. Have you ever noticed how little children will stare at a picture for a long time? This is one form of meditation, and we can do a similar thing. For example, we can meditate on a picture of the crucifixion or on the image of the disfigured face of Jesus. The Catholic Catechism states **"Christians owe it to themselves to develop the desire to meditate regularly, lest they come to resemble the first kinds of soil in the parable of the sower" (Mark 4:4-7, 15-19 NAB)** (#2707).[13]   Don't unnecessarily remain a shallow Christian, increase your love of God through meditation.

One very holy man would pray for four hours without moving, and was an inspiration for all who saw him. Finally, a friend asked him how he prayed. He hesitated to answer such a personal question, but was finally persuaded to share his secret. He stated that like St. John the Apostle he imagined he had his head on Jesus' chest. Then he just relaxed in that position. To me, that is praying like a child, from the heart.

"Practice makes perfect" can also be applied to prayer. In almost every field of endeavor practice is essential. We read of athletes working out 5 or 10 hours a day at their sport. Musicians spend many hours going over the same songs. So, the more we pray, the more relaxed and comfortable we are with prayer as well.

Padre Pio, the holy priest of San Giovanni Rotundo, near Bari Italy, said 40 rosaries a day.

Some people are saying three rosaries daily for world peace. The more we pray, the more we want to pray so long as it is not excessive for us. But the less we pray, the less we want to pray.

When I was on the Island of Grenada in a House of Prayer, one day a week was given totally to prayer by each person who would go off to be alone with the Lord. The other six days were also filled with prayer, but this desert day was different, and it was relatively easy to pray because there was so much time spent with the Lord during the rest of the week.

On my annual retreat, five one hour periods are spent in daily prayer. Then after retreat it is easier to pass three hours daily praying. It is always easier to cut down on prayer time than to increase prayer time.

One religious community has clocks that ring on the quarter hour, and the religious pray a short prayer to consecrate the next 15 minutes to the Lord. That is quite ingenious and practical. If everyone would pray every 15 minutes then we would all be spiritually strong and advanced.

Mohammedans pray seven times a day. At a Catholic college, some Mohammedan students simply put down their prayer mat and prayed towards Mecca. The Catholics were very inspired by this. Would that we would imitate these non-Catholic students and also pray seven times a day.

Here is one simple plan to help evangelize the world. If we would pray during the commercials on television using the mute to cut off the sound, we would pray 20 minutes every hour. Considering that the average American watches television for 5 hours daily, that would add up to 1 hour and 40 minutes per day.

Sacred Scripture portrays Jesus living a life of constant prayer: "In the days when he was in the flesh, he offered prayers and supplications with loud cries and tears to the one who was able to save him from death, and he was heard because of his reverence" (Hebrews 5:7, NAB). Paul was later to say, "Be imitators of me, as I am of Christ" (1 Corinthians 11:1, NAB). Paul was very blessed. We can presume that Paul was able to remain the great apostle because he was a man of great prayer, as Jesus was.

The Early Church lead by the Holy Spirit also stayed in prayer, "They devoted themselves to the teaching of the apostles and to the communal life, to the breaking of the bread and to the prayers" (Acts 2:42, NAB). Paul said, "Pray without ceasing" (I Thessalonians 5:17, NAB). One way to do this is to have the intention of offering every moment of the day as a prayer to the Lord. The ideal for every Christian is to PRAY ALWAYS. Remember, our work and play can and should be a prayer. Let us take this seriously, let us become a prayerful, holy people.

We must find our own level of formal prayer depending on life's circumstances. Priests and religious generally have more time to pray than lay people, but each must find their own schedule. We never pray enough, as a rule. It seems that Jesus and Mary are really stressing prayer in messages given around the world as they say "Pray, Pray, Pray." We are apparently running a race with time to become as intimate with God as we can, and to save by God's grace as many unbelievers as possible. Since we could die at any time, this is not a project we can put off until we retire and have time on our hands. We can't wait until the weekend, because then we definitely would not be praying enough.

So pray with all your might as if all depended on you, and pray simply as a child acknowledging all depends upon God. "Remain in me, as I remain in you. Just as a branch cannot bear fruit on its own unless it remains on the vine" (John. 15:4, NAB). St. Alphonsus Liguori, the great doctor of the Church, tersely stated a great truth about prayer. He said, **"Those who pray will be saved, those who do not pray will be condemned."** Think about the force of that statement. It is one which we should share with our family and friends. If this does not motivate us, then we probably do not fully grasp the concept of or want to think about being condemned, i.e., we could be blocking. If we think this might be the case, then we should pray in childlike absolute faith to God to "remove this and all blockage in Jesus' mighty name".

I have talked with hospital chaplains around the country asking about dying Catholics, and how many of them return to the sacraments on their deathbeds. The priests indicated that most of them do return. One priest, however, drew an interesting distinction. He said that those who generally prayed returned, but those who had given up prayer sometimes did not come back to God. This started me thinking about the importance of encouraging prayer among all people.

The church encourages us to pray in the community (liturgical prayer), e.g., we must go to Mass every Sunday. We can also share in a small group and pray periodically with other people (e.g., a prayer group). Any type of prayer is acceptable. Usually we list prayers of adoration, thanksgiving, petition, and supplication, but there are also prayers of blessing and intercession. These are especially illustrated in the prayer we say before meals, in the Rosary, and in the Psalms.

Lord, please give me the gift of prayer so that I may pray often and well. I desire to become a person of love and communication to please you so much. Let me love to pray often *so that I can hear You* and do Your will. You call us to humility and to become as a little child. I ask You for that grace. It cannot be done without a special grace which I humbly seek from You. Amen

Chapter III

Prayer To Help Another Is An Act Of Kindness

...Since Abraham, intercession – asking on behalf of another – has been characteristic of a heart attuned to God's mercy...In intercession, he who prays looks "not only to his own interests, but also to the interests of others," even to the point of praying for those who do him harm (Luke 23:34, NAB). The first Christian communities lived this form of fellowship intensely. Thus, the Apostle Paul gives them a share in his ministry of preaching the Gospel (1 Thessalonians 5:25, NAB) but also intercedes for them (2 Thessalonians 1:11, NAB). The intercession of Christians knows no boundaries: "for everyone, for kings and for all in authority," for persecutors, for the salvation of those

who reject the Gospel (1 Timothy 2:1, NAB; Romans 12:14;10:1, NAB) (Catechism #2635-6).[14]

We can pray frequently and primarily to the Trinity and still seek intercession from Jesus, Mary, Joseph, and from all of the angels and saints. Prayer to Jesus is "intercessory prayer". Many feel comfortable praying to Jesus for everything they need or want. I know many who pray to Mary extensively for her intercession to Jesus on our behalf. They especially pray to Mary for peace in their lives and in the world. Many people pray (intercessory prayer) to Joseph for the grace of a happy death. Many people pray to St. Michael the Archangel for everyday protection from demonic Powers and Principalities, and also for protection from unusually cruel people. You probably have your own favorite angel and saint to pray to as an intercessor.

Intercessory prayer consists of one person praying for another. Often it is a mother praying for her children. But it may be one of us praying for a friend or relative, or we may ask Our Blessed Mother to pray to the God-Man Jesus for us. We often ask Jesus to pray to Our Father or the Holy Spirit for us. We can pray intercessory prayers for our priests, our parish, our community, our nation, the whole world. No matter which of these we pray for, remember, *God always answers* prayer.

Thomas Merton, the great author and intellectual who lived in the Trappist Monastery in

Gethsemani, Kentucky was giving a group of Prot-estant seminarians a tour of the monastery. He was asked by one of them, "Why do you shut your-self up in this monastery?" Everyone looked at Merton to see what response he would give to this penetrating question. He replied, "I believe in the value of intercessory prayer." He was convinced that his prayers were drawing down God's bless-ings on people. He prayed much and he prayed well.

There are many stories about elderly people who spend their free time in prayer for their grand-children. Is this not the obligation of older people who have gained much wisdom? Unfortunately, young people generally feel the need to make a place for themselves in life, and tend to place prayer at the bottom of their priorities. They feel strong and healthy, and often think they can fix things by themselves, without help. Often they feel money and position are the real powers. To-tally untrue!

Catholics have cloistered monasteries all over the world where religious people spend their lives praying for the Church and for the world. They call down God's graces upon the people so that they will be converted to the Lord Jesus. These religious people spend their whole lives in prayer. Many of us have visited monasteries of men and women, and have noticed how eager and zealous these people are to pray. When I suggest that we pray together after I have given a talk, I see the joy on their faces. Also, when I ask them to lay hands on each other, they are most eager to pray and receive prayer. "The more you pray, the more you want to pray." They spend their life in prayer, and thus they pray well.

We must all pray for the advancement of the Kingdom of God. Our great enemy Satan and his forces are poised, intelligently organized and powerful, and unfortunately all too effective these days. The justice of God requires that grace be made available to save "lost" souls on earth. Jesus prayed the greatest prayer for this, His life, Passion and death; and Mary the next greatest, in her reciprocal suffering. Recently, Jesus gave us *The Chaplet of Mercy*. But we must pray too, to release the treasures of grace stored up by Our Savior. Jesus and Mary **humbly** request our prayers for the advancement of Jesus' kingdom. Jesus certainly has a right to *demand* this of us, but instead He *just pleads* with us to pray and sacrifice so that He can intercede more for sinners and unbelievers. Mary allegedly told the children at Medjugorje that she would pray for us, *but we must pray as well. The unbeliever does not pray*, so we *must* do "their" praying for them. And let us not look merely at others as unbelievers, sometimes we, too, lack faith.

The largest Protestant Church in the world is in Seoul, Korea with almost 750,000 parishioners. Dr. Paul Yongi Cho is the famous pastor who has two "prayer mountains" for his parishioners. They have to make reservations to go there for a week of prayer and fasting. Three thousand people each week on both prayer mountains pray and ask God for the grace to convert Korea. Dr. Cho wanted to have a million parishioners by the year 2,000. With 6,000 people per week praying and fasting, certainly it has happened.

We should "pray over people" by laying on hands whenever possible. We do not need to learn *how* to pray over people; we should do whatever is comfortable in the given situation. It is our own weakness or the demon who tells us that we are not *holy* enough, we don't have time right now, that we shouldn't *even try*. Remember, it is *not we* who do the healing, *it is Jesus*. And we are *not just trying* to pray, **we are praying** – we pray, and God *always, always* answers prayer. We must believe this fully and without any reservation at all. Leave the timing and the answer up to God, but He **always** answers our prayer. The more unworthy we feel, the more humble we are, so don't ever get discouraged. Trust in God's fatherly goodness and power. Trust in Jesus' eagerness to help us, for *He is the eternal angel who comes even before we call*. Immerse yourself in the gentle light and sweet love of the Holy Spirit.

What should you do, then. *You should pray* as your heart dictates, the way you really feel inclined to pray. You may want to hold hands with someone, you may wish to pray with your hands over their head, with hands on their shoulder, do whatever you feel you should do. Also, you may have certain prayers in which you have more faith, more confidence. Use those prayers, your faith counts. But whatever, don't miss the opportunity to pray over somebody, and do pray over everybody who requests it, or if necessary find somebody else more appropriate to pray over them. You will be greatly blessed for these acts of love. Consider the following testimony of a lady that was "prayed over".

"It was Saturday morning and I was taking a shower when I felt a lump on the side of my breast. As I noticed it a fear went through me. I pressed on the lump and pain went through me. My whole left breast hurt and my back, even my whole arm. When I got dressed I told my mom. You could feel it through my clothes. Previously, I had two tumors removed from both of my breasts and never felt pain since then. So, this time around I was uncomfortable with this lump because of the pain.

"For days I was in pain, but in between I had an ear infection and started taking an antibiotic. I felt the lump had gone down a little but wasn't sure. I thought it was wishful thinking. Yet, it was still hurting. I made an appointment to see the doctor. When I did go, he said 'It was an infection in my breast that made my whole breast, back and arm hurt.' He prescribed an antibiotic that was good for that kind of infection. He did say after I finished the medicine, if the lump didn't

46

go away, I would have to have the lump removed. Something inside kept telling me not to have it opened. I prayed over it and also had remembered Fr. DeGrandis was coming into town.

"I went to the healing Mass at Christ the Good Shepherd in Houston. Before going in the mass I walked into the rest room and heard something tell me to ask a certain girl in the rest room to pray for me! Anyway I didn't obey and went into Mass. After Mass, Father said he would pray over everyone. Again, I heard that voice saying, "Ask the girl you saw in the rest room to pray for you. At that time the same girl passed by. I said, 'No ! I want Fr. DeGrandis to pray for me.' So, I went up and when I sat down afterwards, again I heard the voice, 'Ask her to pray for you.' I said, 'OK !' I looked for her and saw her sitting with a friend. I walked up to her and asked if she'd pray for me. Then when she prayed she knew where the lump was. Her praying was very spiritual and a very relaxing, warm feeling. She blessed me. Three days later, the lump was gone.

"A few weeks later Fr. DeGrandis had another healing Mass. At first I looked for this girl, but didn't see her until the mass was over. She was so excited to see me. She said her friend, who had sat with her when she prayed over me, had a message for me. My Blessed Mother had given him a vision of a woman's body organs above the waist and below the neck, and said to him, 'Go tell her (the girl who prayed for me) that they are clean.' Later I learned that the girl had sensed that I was healed three days after she had prayed over me, so she prayed to Jesus to confirm the healing of my breast to Our Blessed Mother. The next day the message was given to her. I also told her at the pew that my lump was gone and I was healed !

"I remember my Dad always reminded me, when I was a young girl, to always pray to Our Lord for anything I needed and I continue to do so. I have been blessed with an earthly father and mother, and my Heavenly Father and Blessed Mother.

"When I was asked if I wanted to write my experience, I felt honored because I knew it had to have come from the Holy Spirit, but yet I felt awkward, not worthy. So, I kept putting it off. I could hear that same voice, saying, 'Buy a composition book. Carry it with you.' I said, 'OK !' but I still kept putting it off. This went on for a few more days.

One morning as I was leaving for work I remembered I had not taken something to the car. When I came back to my room, right on the floor at the door of my room there was my niece's blank composition book. My parents were still asleep and so was my niece. So, I just smiled and said, 'OK! I'll take it with me and write when I can.' I prayed that the Holy Spirit would help me. So, here is my healing, the love my Lord has for me and for anyone that asks" (Paula, Houston, Texas).

As a young seminarian visiting the hospitals in Washington, D.C., I was impressed with the story of a woman who prayed for her husband to come to the Lord before he died. For 24 years she interceded for her spouse. He was in the hospital for an operation and died suddenly. She was depressed about his spiritual condition. The next day the chaplain called her to relate that her husband had called him before he died, and that he was baptized and received into the church. She is a beautiful example of the power of faith and prayer.

Many people can share stories like this, and they should. We are often too reticent about the grace of God working in our lives. Tell others what the Lord has done for you because people are looking for inspiration and hope. It is certain that the Holy Spirit is working in our lives more than we realize and He wants us to bear fruit in our spiritual lives.

Often I have heard people give witness of their conversion back to the Lord Jesus. There are many details, but what I always look for is a person who has prayed for this individual's conversion. You will always find that *someone* prayed for this person to receive the gift of conversion. Perhaps *your* father or mother, grandmother, brother or sister has been praying for *you* to turn to the Lord. Maybe *you* are praying for a family member to surrender to the Lord Jesus; that is intercession.

These days, most people have someone in their immediate family or one of their relatives who seem well on their way to Hell as far as they can humanly judge. You must pray very hard for the salvation of that soul. Never give up; you are also being blessed as you pray for them. You are showing great love and solicitude as you are growing in love. And don't forget, "... love covers a multitude of sins" (I Peter 4:8, NAB), including *our* sins.

We need to re-emphasize the Golden Rule, to teach it to our young people through example. "Do to others whatever you would have them do to you. This is the law and the prophets" (Matthew 7:12, NAB). These are golden opportunities for us to become more holy, to cover our sins. *We all need to cover our sins by love and charity. If we don't realize this now, we surely will at some time in the future!*

At a First Communion, the priest asked the first communicants to stand and look at the people in the church. He said, "Jesus now wants you to love all these people." This was a marvelous insight. Jesus gives Himself to us so that we can love everyone. That is a gigantic order, but we should try to do the best we can for the rest of our lives. Prayer is the invaluable help.

"The Christopher News Notes"[15] recently had an issue on "keeping the Golden Rule". The insights were fascinating. They are well worth repeating here:

"Show Genuine Appreciation"

Years ago I worked with a priest who always said 'Thank you' when you helped him. He changed my life in the way I deal with others.

"Give Compliments"

There is so much that is good around us, but we often miss the joy and pleasure by being negative. A foreigner once said what she liked most about the United States is that most things work. I was surprised, but in her country, many things don't work: the telephone, the bus, the planes, medical services, etc. We need to constantly compliment the service people around us for their excellent work.

"Point Out The Good In Others"

One priest preaches that we should try to say one good thing about each person we meet. That could revolutionize our society. Try it.

"Act Cheerfully"

This is a matter of self-discipline. It is easy to spew our negativity on people, but Jesus calls us to 'Love one another', to give the best we have. One day, Mother Theresa said to a nun 'Go back to bed, you look so unhappy.' Mother wanted her to be cheerful. Paul says: *"Rejoice in the Lord always, I say it again, rejoice"* (Philippians. 4:4, NAB).

"Practice Kindness"

Traveling a lot, I have wonderful opportunities to be kind when I see an older person carrying heavy luggage. It is so easy for me to take it to the gate. Sometimes I miss the opportunity, but frequently I am able to render this helpful service.

"Forgive"

Listen to this testimony:

'After 25 years of bearing a grudge against an alcoholic stepfather (who committed suicide), I decided with a simple prayer to forgive him. I used to hate him and felt glad of the day he died (as Baptist children used to tease me about his drinking), but after praying for forgiveness, I discovered that I had a kind heart towards him. I pictured being in heaven and seeing my stepfather's entrance. I found myself happy to see him. I learned from this circumstance that not only can one forgive the past, but one can be reconciled with it also. I marvel how God is able to transcend time.' "

A good prayer life will impel us to begin to reach out in love and be people who live the "Golden Rule". Every night we should examine our conscience. "How did I practice love today and keep the Golden Rule, and where did I miss an opportunity? This will keep us sensitive to the Christian obligations of charity. "So faith, hope, love remain, these three, but the greatest of these is love" (1 Corinthians 13:13, NAB).

A few years ago, a woman in New Orleans had two daughters on drugs, and one was almost killed when she was shot near the heart. The mother prayed at every free moment for her children. I would often see her praying the Psalms as intercession for her poor, wandering offspring. Finally, after three years, both were free of drugs and living a normal life. That picture of the praying mother stays with me as a symbol of the power of intercession. "Faith moves mountains."

Some would say there are impossible situations in their families that cannot be changed by prayer and faith. Many of us feel that way from time to time. The following excerpts have been an example of what skepticism can lead to:

> **"The Airplane**-'The (flying) machine will eventually be fast; they will be used in sport, but are not to be thought of as commercial carriers.' *Octave Chanute*, 1904.
> **"The Automobile**-'The ordinary *horseless carriage* is at present a luxury for the wealthy; and although its price will

probably fall in the future, it will never come into as common use as the bicycle.' *The Literary Digest*, Oct. 14, 1889.

"Electricity in the Home-'Just as certain as death, [George] Westinghouse will kill a customer within six months after he puts in a system of any size.' - Thomas Edison.

"The Grand Canyon-' [It] is, of course, altogether valueless... Ours has been the first, and will doubtless be the last party of whites to visit this profitless locality.' -Lt. Joseph C. Ives, Corps of Topological Engineers, 1861.

"Lunar Landing-'Landing and moving around on the moon offer so many serious problems for human beings that it may take science another 200 years to lick them.' *Science Digest,* August 1948.

"Surgery-'The abdomen, the chest, and the brain will be forever shut from the intrusion of the wise and humane surgeon. -Sir John Erichsen, 1873.

"Television-'While theoretically and technically television may be feasible, commercially and financially I consider it an impossibility, a development of which we need waste little time dreaming.'-Lee DeForest, 1926.

"X-Ray-'X-rays are a hoax.'-Lord Kelvin, who seemed to have a corner on the wrong-headed one-liner during his time, 'Aircraft flight is impossible," he said, as well as, 'Radio has no future.' " [16]

We need to pray more for corporate America. The world is becoming so pagan that it is difficult for Christians to work in the corporate world. When so many are doing immoral things, it puts severe pressure on the conscientious Christian who is sincerely trying to function as a decent human being. One secretary told her boss she would not lie for him, and he promptly fired her. Another nurse refused to participate in abortions in her hospital, and her supervisor said she would assist or get fired. Most people are aware of similar situations.

Our income tax is often a temptation for many people to lie and cheat. We must resist the temptation. It is very difficult for a person to jeopardize his or her income. I have seen it "tear" people apart so they actually got sick over a situation. They wanted to do what was right as a Christian, but would suffer great loss if they did so. Perhaps we are being called to a type of "martyrdom", that is, a "witnessing" to the Lord.

Lord, help us in our battle, be our intercessor. Give me a greater love for you so that I can pray often for people and situations and be a great intercessor. Help me to pray for myself and for others; for the conversion of unbelievers; for souls in Purgatory; and for the sick, the suffering, and the dying. Amen

Chapter IV

Prayer Builds On Forgiveness And Healing

Jesus was absolute when it came to forgiveness. In speaking to the apostles on how to pray, He taught them the "Our Father", and then He added: "If you forgive others their transgressions, your heavenly Father will forgive you. But if you do not forgive others, neither will your Father forgive your transgressions" (Matthew 6:14&15, NAB). Jesus provided the ultimate example of forgiveness when, in utter agony on the cross, He uttered **the most precious words ever spoken**, **"...Father, forgive them, for they know not what they do..."** (Luke 23:34, NAB). Our Father heard and honored these sweetest words. Jesus was pleading for all of mankind, and He still is, until the end of time.

These are very strong statements by Jesus. We can say in a sense that "forgiveness comes before prayer" because unforgiveness can weaken the power of prayer. However, the more we pray, the more we can forgive. And the deeper our forgiveness, the more powerful our prayer. Note the following statement in the Catholic Catechism[17]:

> **From the sermon on the mount onwards, Jesus insists on conversion of the heart:** *reconciliation with one's brother before presenting an offering on the altar, love of enemies, and prayer for persecutors*, **prayer to the Father in secret, not heaping up empty phrases,** *powerful forgiveness from the depths of the heart*, **purity of heart, and seeking the Kingdom before all else.** (#2608)

Forgiveness requires love. These two acts of the will, "forgiveness and love," correlate and are proportional. In the Gospel of John we read the most important lines in the New Testament. God is described in three words by the Holy Spirit, "...God is Love..." (1 John 4:16, NAB). That means the nature of God is love. Our whole life is a matter of receiving and giving love. The role of a Christian is "...Love one another as I love you" (John 15:12, NAB). Where there is true love, there is true forgiveness. Since God's forgiveness is without limit, ours should be also. Peter thought he was doing well in understanding Jesus' teaching when he said: "...Lord, if my brother sins against me, how often must I forgive Him? As many as seven times? Jesus answered, 'I say to you, not seven times, but seventy-seven times'"

(Matthew 18:21- 22, NAB).

Peter felt he was being liberal or at least reasonable in forgiving seven times, perhaps because scripture says the just man falls seven times a day. In biblical days the number seven represented completeness, so Peter probably thought that was sufficient. Rather, Jesus shows Peter the love of His Father, and tells him that **there is no limit to how many times and how much we should forgive**. This is perhaps one of the most difficult hurdles for us.

Almost everyone has had at least one serious and severely damaging incident which they struggle with, and find almost impossible to forgive. That is why the Gospel is so important in our lives. We find happiness to the extent we live the Gospel of Jesus Christ. Assuming that unforgiveness is a great obstacle to prayer and could jeopardize my future with the Lord, how can I forgive those who hurt me so badly that I become extremely angry when I think of them and the situation? I think I forgave them, but when their names are mentioned or they do something that I don't like, great anger wells up inside of me.

This is such a complex issue because all of us carry deep, buried painful experiences for which there is anger and perhaps bitterness. We are not aware of it, but it still can affect us. Yet all of us are called upon to keep our hearts and minds clear and pure from festering mental sores, bitterness, resentment, and unforgiveness.

The answer is, **you may never be able to for-**

give them, not **by yourself**. At least in these instances you must appeal to Jesus, Mary and Joseph for help, there is no other way. The most important fact about forgiveness is that it is an act of the will, not a feeling. If you pray consistently for a person, that is an act of the will and you are clearing away blocks to the Holy Spirit.

When people cannot or do not forgive, we see disastrous results. All the wars that are being waged in different parts of the world ultimately come down to a failure to forgive. Some hatreds have gone on for thousands of years. There seems to be no hope that they will ever be healed. Hatred leads to family feuds, injustice, sometimes murder. However, revenge cannot be enacted by a good Christian. Only forgiveness heals wounds.

Don't forget to forgive yourself, also. Like God, we too must love ourselves. As sinners who have consciences, we carry a certain amount of guilt. We also have spiritual wounds. Unforgiveness of ourselves can be a complete block to the deep inner healing that we would ordinarily receive through Eucharist and prayer. We need to forgive "ourselves" daily as well. This process must be ongoing for the rest of our lives.

The following is a forgiveness prayer that has helped thousands of people. I like to encourage people to say it for 30 days (at least) and to write down the names of people who come to mind as the prayer is recited. Usually, more names will come mightily after 15 days of reciting the prayer.

It is the common experience of people that

great healing follows. We have seen cancer, heart problems, high blood pressure, and lupus healed. Use it with people who are having any type of problem.

Forgiveness Prayer

The following prayer covers most of the significant areas of forgiveness. Often, such a prayer will bring to mind other areas that need forgiveness. Let the Holy Spirit move freely and guide your mind to persons or groups that you need to forgive.

Lord Jesus Christ, I ask today to forgive everyone in my life. I know that You will give me the strength to forgive and I thank You that You love me more than I love myself and want my happiness more than I desire it for myself.

Father, I forgive You for the times death has come into the family, hard times, financial difficulties, or that I thought were punishments sent by You and people said, "It's God's will," and I became bitter and resentful toward You. Purify my heart and mind today.

Lord, I forgive MYSELF for my sins, faults and failings, for all that is bad in myself or that I think is bad, I forgive myself. For any delvings in superstition, using Ouija boards, horoscopes, going to seances, using fortune

telling or wearing lucky charms, I reject all that superstition and choose You alone as my Lord and Savior. Fill me with Your Holy Spirit.

I further forgive myself for taking Your name in vain, for not worshipping You by attending church, for hurting my parents, getting drunk, for sins against purity, bad books, bad movies, fornication, adultery, homosexual activity. You have forgiven me; today I forgive myself.

For abortion, stealing, lying, defrauding, hurting peoples' reputation, I forgive myself.

I truly forgive my MOTHER. I forgive her for all the times she hurt me, she resented me, she was angry with me and for all the times she punished me. I forgive her for the times she preferred my brothers and sisters to me. I forgive her for the times she told me I was dumb, ugly, stupid, the worst of the children or that I cost the family a lot of money. For the times she told me I was unwanted, an accident, a mistake or not what she expected, I forgive her. Even for her dying, I forgive her.

I forgive my FATHER. I forgive him for any non-support, any lack of love, affection or attention. I forgive him for any lack of time, for not giving me his companionship, for his drinking, for arguing and fighting with my mother or the other children. For his severe punishments, for desertion, for being away from home, for divorcing my mother or for any running around, I do forgive him. If he died when I was young, or older, I do forgive him for leaving me.

Lord, I extend forgiveness to my SISTERS AND BROTHERS. I forgive those who rejected me, lied about me, hated me, resented me, competed for my parents' love, hurt me, physically harmed me. For those who were too severe on me, punished me or made my life unpleasant in any way, I do forgive them.

Lord, I forgive my SPOUSE for lack of love, affection, consideration, support, attention, communication, for faults, failings, weaknesses and those other acts or words that hurt or disturbed me.

Jesus, I forgive my CHILDREN for their lack of respect, obedience, love, attention, support, warmth, understanding, for their bad habits, falling away from the church, any bad actions which disturb me.

My God, I forgive my IN-LAWS, MY MOTHER-IN-LAW, FATHER-IN-LAW, SON/DAUGHTER-IN-LAW

AND OTHER RELATIVES by marriage who treat my family with a lack of love. For all their words, thoughts, actions or omissions which injure and cause pain, I forgive them.

Please help me to forgive my RELATIVES, my grandmother and grandfather, aunts, uncles, nieces, nephews, cousins, who may have interfered in our family, been possessive of my parents, who may have caused confusion or turned one parent against the other.

Jesus, help me to forgive my CO-WORKERS who are disagreeable or make life miserable for me. For those who push their work off on me, gossip about me, won't cooperate with me, try to take my job, I do forgive them.

My NEIGHBORS need to be forgiven, Lord. For all their prejudice, noise, letting their property run down, not tying up their dogs who run through my yard, not taking in their trash barrels, and generally running down the neighborhood, I do forgive them.

I now forgive all PRIESTS AND NUNS, MY PARISH, PARISH COUNCIL, PARISH ORGANIZATIONS, MY PASTOR, THE BISHOP, THE POPE, AND THE ROMAN CATHOLIC CHURCH for their lack of support, affirmation, for bad sermons, pettiness,

63

lack of friendliness, not providing me or my family with the inspiration we needed, for any hurts they have inflicted on me or my family, even in the distant past, I forgive them today.

Lord, I forgive all those who are of different PERSUASIONS, those of opposite political views who have attacked me, ridiculed me, discriminated against me, made fun of me, economically hurt me.

I forgive those of different religious DENOMINATIONS who have tried to convert me, harassed me, attacked me, argued with me, tried to force their views on me.

Those who have harmed me ETHNICALLY, have discriminated against me, mocked me, made jokes about my race or nationality, hurt my family physically, emotionally or economically, I do forgive them today.

Lord, I forgive all PROFESSIONAL PEOPLE who have hurt me in any way: doctors, nurses, lawyers, judges, politicians and civil servants. I forgive all service people: policemen, firemen, bus drivers, hospital workers and especially repairmen who have taken advantage of me in their work.

Lord, I forgive my EMPLOYER for not paying me enough money, for not appreciating my work, for being unkind and unreasonable, for being angry or unfriendly, for not promoting me, and for not complimenting me on my work.

Lord, I forgive my SCHOOL TEACHERS AND INSTRUCTORS of the past as well as the present. For those who punished me, humiliated me, insulted me, treated me unjustly, made fun of me, called me dumb or stupid, made me stay after school, I truly forgive them today.

Lord, I forgive my FRIENDS who have let me down, lost contact with me, do not support me, were not available when I needed help, borrowed money and did not return it, gossiped about me.

Lord Jesus, I especially pray for the grace of forgiveness for that ONE PERSON in life who has HURT ME THE MOST. I ask help to forgive the one whom I consider my greatest enemy, the one who is hardest to forgive, or the one whom I said I will never forgive.

Lord, I beg pardon of all these people for the hurt I have inflicted on them, especially my mother and father, and my marriage partner. I am especially sorry for the three greatest hurts I have inflicted on each.

Thank You, Jesus, that I am being freed of the evil of unforgiveness. Let Your Holy Spirit fill me with light, and let every dark area of my mind be enlightened. AMEN.

NOTE:

FORGIVENESS IS AN ACT OF THE WILL, NOT A FEELING. IF WE PRAY FOR A PERSON, WE CAN BE ASSURED THAT WE HAVE FORGIVEN THAT PERSON.

TO HELP ACCEPT AN INDIVIDUAL AND OPEN OURSELVES TO A PARTICULAR PERSON MORE, VISUALIZE HIM WITH THE LORD JESUS, AND SAY TO THE LORD, "I LOVE HIM BECAUSE YOU LOVE HIM."

FORGIVENESS IS A LIFE-LONG OBLIGATION.

WE NEED TO FORGIVE THOSE WHO HURT OR INJURE US EVERY DAY.

"This is my commandment: love one another as I love you" (John 15:12, NAB).

We can summarize the teaching on forgiveness with these thoughts:

RECALL THE TEN MOST PAINFUL EVENTS OF YOUR LIFE.

RELEASE THEM TO THE LORD IN PRAYER AS YOU IMAGINE YOUR-

SELF UNDER THE CROSS LOOKING
UP AT THE DYING JESUS.

RECORD THE NAMES THAT
COME TO MIND AS YOU SAY THE
FORGIVENESS PRAYER.

REJOICE THAT YOU ARE BEING
HEALED AS YOU FORGIVE.

REFLECT ON THE TEMPTATION
TO FEEL YOU HAVE NOT FORGIVEN
WHEN STRONG FEELINGS ARISE IN
YOUR HEART.

RECOVER YOUR PEACE AND
JOY AS YOU LIVE THE GOSPEL OF
YOUR FATHER'S LOVE.

The healing power of forgiveness overflows
in the next testimony, "Don't Let It End this Way":

" 'Janie, this is Sue Kidd, a registered
nurse at the hospital. I'm calling about
your father. He was admitted today with
a slight heart attack and . . .'

" 'No!' she screamed into the phone,
startling me. 'He's not dying is he?' It
was more a painful plea than a question.

" 'His condition is stable at the
moment,' I said, trying hard to sound
convincing.

"Silence. I bit my lip.

" 'You must not let him die!' she said.
Her voice was so utterly compelling that
my hand trembled on the phone.

" 'He is getting the very best care.'

" 'But you don't understand,' she pleaded. 'My daddy and I haven't spoken in almost a year. We had a terrible argument on my twenty-first birthday, over my boyfriend.'

"I ran out of the house. I . . . I haven't been back. All these months I've wanted to go to him for forgiveness. The last thing I said to him was, 'I hate you.'"

"Her voice cracked and I heard her heave great agonizing sobs. I sat, listening, tears burning my eyes. A father and a daughter, so lost to each other! Then I was thinking of my own father, many miles away. It had been so long since I had said I love you.

"As Janie struggled to control her tears, I breathed a prayer. 'Please God, let this daughter find forgiveness.'

" 'I'm coming, now! I'll be there in thirty minutes,' she said. Click. She had hung up.

"I tried to busy myself with a stack of charts on the desk. I couldn't concentrate. Room 712. I knew I had to get back to 712. I hurried down the hall nearly in a run. I opened the door.

"Mr. Williams laid unmoving. I reached for his pulse. There was none.

" 'Code ninety-nine. Room 712. Code ninety-nine. Stat.' The alert was shooting through the hospital within seconds after I called the switchboard through the intercom by the bed.

"Mr. Williams had had a cardiac arrest.

"With lightning speed I leveled the bed and bent over his mouth, breathing air into his lungs. I positioned my head over his chest and compressed. One, two, three. I tried to count. At fifteen, I moved back to his mouth and breathed as deeply as I could. Where was help? Again I compressed and breathed. Compressed and breathed. He could not die!

" 'Oh, God,' I prayed. 'His daughter is coming. Don't let it end this way.'

"The door burst open. Doctors and nurses poured into the room, pushing emergency equipment.

"A doctor took over the manual compression of the heart. A tube was inserted through his mouth as an airway. Nurses plunged syringes of medicine into the intravenous tubing.

"I connected the heart monitor. Nothing. Not a beat. My own heart pounded. 'God, don't let it end like this. Not in bitterness and hatred. His daughter is coming. Let her find peace.'

" 'Stand back,' cried a doctor. I handed him the paddles for the electrical shock to the heart. He placed them on Mr. William's chest. Over and over we tried. But nothing. No response. Mr. Williams was dead.

"A nurse unplugged the oxygen. The gurgling stopped. One by one they left, grim and silent.

"How could this happen? How? I stood by his bed, stunned. A cold wind rattled the window, pelting the panes with snow. Outside -- everywhere -- seemed a bed of blackness, cold and dark. How could I face his daughter?

"When I left the room, I saw her against the wall by a water fountain. A doctor, who had been in 712 only moments before, stood at her side, talking to her, gripping her elbow. Then he moved on, leaving her slumped against the wall.

"Such pathetic hurt reflected from her face. Such wounded eyes. She knew. The doctor had told her that her father was gone.

"I took her hand and let her into the nurses' lounge. We sat on little green stools, neither saying a word. She stared straight ahead at a pharmaceutical calendar, glass-faced, almost breakable-looking.

" 'Janie, I'm so, so sorry,' I said. It was pitifully inadequate. 'I never hated him, you know. I loved him,' she said. God, please help her, I prayed. Suddenly she whirled toward me. 'I want to see him.'

"My first thought was, why put yourself through more pain? Seeing him will only make it worse. But I got up and wrapped my arm around her. We walked slowly down the corridor to 712. Outside the door I squeezed her hand, wishing she would change her mind about going inside. She pushed open the door.

"We moved to the bed, huddled together, taking small steps in unison, Janie leaned over the bed and buried her face in the sheets.

I tried not to look at her, at this sad, sad good-bye. I backed against the bedside table. My hand fell upon a scrap of yellow paper. I picked it up. I read.

" 'My dearest Janie, I forgive you. I pray you will also forgive me. I know that you love me. I love you, too. Daddy'".

"The note was shaking in my hands as I thrust it toward Janie. She read it once. Then twice. Her tormented face grew radiant. Peace began to glisten in her eyes. She hugged the scrap of paper to her breast.

" 'Thank you, God,' I whispered, looking up at the window. A few crystal stars blinked through the blackness. A snowflake hit the window and melted away, gone forever.

"Life seemed as fragile as a snowflake on the window. But thank you, God, the relationships, sometimes fragile as snow-flakes, can be mended together again. But there is not a moment to spare.

"I crept from the room and hurried to the phone. I would call my own father. I would say, 'I love you.' "[18]

Prayer brings healing from God for our spirit, our mind, and sometimes our body. Many Catholics recoil when one mentions the word "healing" but the scriptures mention it frequently. "These signs will accompany those who believe . . . They will lay hands on the sick and they will recover" (Mark 16:17-18, NAB). A simple definition often diffuses anxiety about this mysterious term: "**Healing is simply an answer to prayer**".

People of deep and frequent prayer report many beautiful and dramatic answers to their petitions from the Lord Jesus. That is the way it should be. We are in union with the Lord through Grace, His presence within us. "If you remain in me and my words remain in you, ask for whatever you want and it will be done for you" (John 15:7, NAB). The more we pray, the more we receive. Most Christians can relate incidents of answered prayer. Some have experienced some type of healing.

Jean Hilliard's car got stuck in a northern Minnesota snowstorm with temperature at minus twenty-five and wind gusts up to 50 miles an hour. She trudged to a farmhouse and blacked out.

Her testimony helps clarify the principle that "prayer brings healing from God for our spirit, our mind, and sometimes our body":

She Was Frozen Solid

"I grabbed my purse and the car keys, threw on my green waist-length parka and started toward the door. Mom called, 'Jean, aren't you going to take your boots and snowmobile pants? It's supposed to get colder tonight.'

"I'd lived on a farm in northern Minnesota all my life and was used to cold weather. 'I'll be fine, Mom. Just driving into town to meet some friends. It's not that cold.'

"It was December 20, 1980. I was 19 years old and thought cowboy boots and blue jeans were more appropriate than warm clothing for a night out with friends. Besides, I had no idea that the temperature would plummet to 25 degrees below zero with gusts of 50 miles an hour.

"Around midnight, after a fun evening in Fosston with my friends, I was driving home alone in Dad's big white Ford LTD. The snow sparkled festively in the beams of my headlights. I decided to take the old country road because it was a few miles shorter than the blacktop. Besides, I had always loved that road. It meandered through a forest of tall pines. Every couple of miles a house or a farm dotted the landscape, but the rest was pure picture-postcard scenery -- icy-blue Minnesota lakes, tall trees and the narrow, winding, hilly gravel road.

"I didn't see the patch of ice in the middle of the road because of the new snow. Before I knew what was happening, the car skidded off to the side, and the front wheel slid precariously close to a ditch. I tried to back up slowly, but the tires were spinning. When I put the car in forward gear the front tire slipped off the shoulder, and the car became helplessly marooned.

"I wasn't frightened, but I sure was disgusted! I could just hear Dad's voice when he found out what I'd done with his good car.

"I knew there was a house a half mile or so ahead, so I got out of the car and stomped off down the road, forgetting my hat on the front seat.

"I was steaming over the mess I had gotten myself into, and my anger kept me warm for a few hundred feet. The wind forced me to zip my jacket collar up over my nose and mouth. I shoved my hands deep into my pockets and dug into the snow with my pointy-toed leather cowboy boots.

"I walked on a little farther and then remembered Wally's place, in the opposite direction. It should be just a half mile or so, I thought. Wally was an acquaintance of my folks. I knew he had a four-wheel-drive truck and could pull my car out of the ditch.

"As I passed the car, I felt like kicking the tire, but I trudged on. After a half mile or so, I passed a house. It was dark and there were no tracks in the driveway. Probably out of town, I thought. I walked on another half mile or more. The next house was also dark and the driveway filled with snow without a tire track to be seen.

"I pressed on. The wind whipped through the pines. My feet were starting to bother me. My dressy cowboy boots were not meant for hiking. Why hadn't I listened to Mom and taken my warmer boots?

"Where was Wally's house, anyway? I thought it was just over the next hill. I kept walking, but the front of my legs, protected only by my thin blue jeans, were aching from the cold. Down another hill. Why did I take the shortcut? At least on the blacktop there would be cars on the road this time of night.

"I struggled up another hill. Finally, I thought I saw Wally's farm in the distance. Yes! There was the long lane leading to his house. I was breathing harder. And then . . I blacked out.

"Although I don't remember it, apparently I half walked, half stumbled, falling at times, down the long lane. I crawled the last hundred feet or so on my hands and knees, but I don't remember doing that either.

"By now, the windchill was 70 to 80 degrees below zero. Right at Wally's front door I collapsed and fell face forward into the snow. And that's where I lay all night.

"The next morning Wally came out his front door just before seven o'clock. Normally he didn't go to work until eight, but thank God, he decided to go in early that morning. Wally saw my body in the snow, leaned down and tried to find a pulse. There was none. My swollen face was a gray, ashen color. My eyes were frozen open. I wasn't breathing.

"Wally still doesn't know how he managed to pick me up and get me into his car. He said it was like struggling with a 120-pound log or a big piece of meat out of the freezer.

"At the hospital in Fosston, Wally yelled through the emergency room doorway for help. He picked me up under my arms while a couple of nurses lifted me by my ankles. My body didn't bend anywhere.

"As they were putting me on a stretcher, one nurse exclaimed, 'She's frozen solid!' Another nurse, the mother of one of my best friends, said, 'It's Jean Hilliard! I recognize her blond hair and green jacket.'

"Rosie Erickson, who worked in bookkeeping, ran out into the hall when she heard the commotion. She leaned over my body. 'It's a moaning sound . . . coming from her throat. Listen!'

"I was wheeled into the emergency room. Dr. George Sather, our family doctor, was on duty that morning. With his stethoscope he was unable to hear any breathing or a heartbeat. Then he attached a heart monitor, which picked up a very slow, faint heartbeat. A cardiologist said it seemed to be 'a dying heart.'

" 'We have to get these boots off! Bring some blankets! She's still alive!' My boots and jacket were the only items of clothing they could get off immediately. The rest of my clothes were frozen on.

"When they cut off my jeans, the staff saw that my feet were black and there were black areas on my legs and lower back. The tissue damage seemed so severe that when my parents arrived Dr. Sather told them that if I did live, my legs might have to be amputated.

"Dr. Sather ordered oxygen, and a

nurse suggested trying Aqua-K-pads. Just the day before, a new kind of water-filled heating pad had arrived at the hospital and quickly they were unpacked. Fortunately the only nurse on the staff who knew how to connect them to the special water-filled machines was on duty and she directed the procedure.

"My body was frozen so hard that the staff couldn't pierce my skin with a hypo-dermic needle. There was no way at first to give me any medication to speed the thawing process or to prevent infection. But the medical team didn't know what Rosie Erickson was about to do.

"Rosie found my parents in the hall. 'Mr. and Mrs. Hilliard, do you mind if I put Jean on the prayer chain at our church?'

"Mom answered quickly: 'Yes . . . please do!'

"Mrs. Erickson hurried to her office and made a phone call to the prayer chain chairman at the Baptist church where her husband is the pastor. The prayer chain was set in motion.

"My heart started beating slightly faster. Even though still far slower than the normal rate of about 72 times a minute, the doctors were overjoyed. I started breathing on my own.

"The prayer chain was lengthening.

Mrs. Erickson called the pastors of the Lutheran, Catholic, Methodist and Bethel Assembly churches in Fosston. They, in turn, called the chairmen of their prayer chain groups, who passed the word along.

"During the first hours that the prayer chain was underway, my legs and feet, instead of getting darker as Dr. Sather expected, started to lighten and regain their natural color. One after another, the doctors and nurses filed in to marvel at the pinkish tinge appearing at the line of demarcation where the darkness started on my upper thighs -- the place where Dr. Sather said he thought they might have to amputate.

"The prayer chain spread to the nearby towns of Crookston and Bemidji, and into Grand Forks, N.D. Soon hundreds, then thousands of people were aware that a young woman had been brought in to the Fosston hospital frozen solid and was in desperate need of God's miraculous healing.

"One of the nurses, on her way to get more blankets, poked her head into Mrs. Erickson's doorway and said, 'Jean might make it. Her legs are starting to regain color at the top. And her heart is beating stronger.'

"Mrs. Erickson looked up at the clock and thought, the prayer chain is in full swing now. God is answering those prayers already. Of course she's going to make it!

"At that moment the whole attitude in my hospital room changed. Now, instead of 'She probably won't survive' the feeling was 'Perhaps she'll live, but she will surely lose her legs from the knees down.'

"Before noon that day I stirred and moaned a word that sounded like 'Mom.' My mother and oldest sister, Sandra, stayed near my bed, holding, squeezing and patting my hands. 'Jean, wake up! Jeannie, can you hear me?'

"All over the area the prayer chain was continuing. By mid-afternoon I woke up and started thrashing in bed. The doctors told me later that I moaned and yelled so much that they were convinced I would have severe brain damage.

"All day the nurses and doctors watched in amazement as the blackness in my legs and feet disappeared inch by inch. By late afternoon Dr. Sather thought that perhaps only my feet might have to be amputated. A few hours later he was astounded to realize that perhaps it would be just my toes.

"In the end I did not lose any part of my body! Normal color and circulation came back even to the blackest parts of my legs, feet and toes.

"Dr. Sather had also thought he would have to do numerous skin grafts where huge blisters covered my toes. But these places healed too without skin grafting.

"Indeed, after watching my body become whole again, I am convinced that a miracle did occur. Even Dr. Sather said, 'I just took care of her. God healed her.'

"The doctors kept me in the hospital for seven weeks to make sure of my recovery from frostbite, and to lessen the possibility of any infection. During that entire time I never once experienced any fear. I'm convinced it was the prayer chain that kept me calm and filled me with a positive faith that I would be healed.

"Thousands of people I didn't even know bombarded heaven with powerful prayer requests in my behalf, and against all medical odds I not only lived, I survived as a completely normal, whole human being without even so much as a skin graft. In fact, unlike most other people who have suffered from frostbite, I now experience no ill effects from the cold.

"As one minister reminded me when we later spoke of the prayer chain, we as God's children have been commanded to 'Pray without ceasing' (1 Thessalonians 5:17, NAB).

"All those people praying unceasingly for me -- I'm sure that was what caused my miracle."[19]

Lord, give me a gift of a "forgiving heart" so I can be as You - always loving unconditionally. I hear You calling to me to be humble and to forgive those who have hurt me. Thank You for the grace of forgiveness to others and healing of my heart. Amen

Chapter V

Prayer Changes Us, Not God

"…My Father, if it is possible, let this cup pass from me; yet, not as I will, but as you will" (Matthew 26:39 NAB).

Some people object to praying because they think we are trying to change God with our intentions. Really, prayer is the way through which "we" are changed. This is clear when a spouse dies and the other partner is in deep pain. Prayer can bring healing through acceptance of what cannot be changed.

A veteran with one leg was entering a shrine and a bystander said, "Is he asking for a new leg?" The man turned and said, "I am asking for the grace of acceptance."

Some writers compare us to iron. We are immersed in the fire of God's love through prayer, and then like a red hot iron, God can best shape us. Without the fire of divine love, we would be inflexible. We are in a sense like a wax candle. When cold, it is inflexible, but heated, it can be easily bent.

Many of the problems in life are those of acceptance. We have to accept ourselves, our parents and sometimes even our life situations. We often rebel and try to change them. By prayer, we are often able to accept others and situations as they are. Who among us would not like to change many aspects of our lives. But by grace, we are able to find peace and fulfillment in accepting what cannot be changed.

When a baby is born and grows, it can only think in terms of "me". It grabs everything for itself. As the baby grows to adulthood and into marriage, the emphasis is on "ours" and on giving. Jesus says, "...It is more blessed to give than receive" (Acts 20:35, NAB). So maturity means giving to find fulfillment. The more we yield to God's will, the happier we become.

The ultimate change is death. There comes a time when we have to accept the final act of life, the dying process. Often, I have seen people pray their way to gentle acceptance and experience a joyful death. A joyful death is a great victory over death, an extension of that won by Our Savior on the cross 2,000 years ago. Prayer changes even the most "final" things.

There was a woman missionary in China who was very sick. Through prayer she finally said "Lord, whatever you want is what I want, sickness or health." She surrendered and was instantly healed. Prayer changed her from anxiously wanting healing to gentle acceptance. Catherine Marshall, the famous writer, was sick in bed reading this story. She also surrendered and was instantly healed. Prayer brings us to surrender, so God's grace can work more powerfully.

Shari Smyth of South Salem, New York illustrates in her story how God's grace works miracles in the human heart and changes us.

I Want a Miracle

"My son, Patrick, was severely handicapped, both physically and mentally, with cerebral palsy. He was one of triplet boys that had been born a month and a half prematurely. The other sons had not survived. One died the day after birth; the other three months later, at home. Crib death. My grief for them was still raw when I learned that Patrick was profoundly retarded. I was told he would never walk, never sit up by himself, never be toilet trained, never speak. But I wanted a miracle.

"He was two when I read about a healing service in a flyer at church. Hoping to discourage me, my husband, Whitney said he couldn't make the trip to Pittsburgh with us.

" 'I'll take Patrick by myself,' I told him, 'We'll fly.' Whitney shook his head.

" 'Shari, I want our son whole as much as you do, but if God wanted to heal

Patrick, he could do it here.' But Whitney finally relented.

"I reserved a seat on a flight to Pittsburgh, and one morning a week later, while it was still dark, I drove to the airport. Patrick was in back strapped in his special car seat.

"He had a head full of blond curls and a smile that lit up a room. He could roll over and move across the floor in a fish-like movement, but I pictured him walking, holding up his arms to me, learning to talk. I couldn't let go of that image. I begged and bargained with God. Going to Pittsburgh was putting my faith into action. I didn't have a drop of doubt that summer morning.

"It was just getting light when I parked the car and carried Patrick to the terminal. He was heavy and cumbersome. We boarded the plane. During the short bumpy ride I whispered into my son's ear how much I loved him. It tickled him and he giggled. He also made the strange noises I knew as happy sounds. Nearby passengers shifted in their seats uncomfortably. I understood, knowing their stares held sympathy, as well as fear. Once, what seemed like light-years ago, I had said that the two things I couldn't take would be losing a child or having one who was profoundly handicapped.

"I buried my face in Patrick's silky hair, loving him with an ache that was almost unbearable. Even so, I wanted a miracle. I leaned my head against the double-paned window and stared at the clouds. Behind me a child looking at the same view called, 'The sky has hair, Mummy.' I clenched my jaw, fastening my faith like a seat belt. I had heard amazing things about these healing services.

"The intercom crackled. 'Ladies and gentlemen, we will be landing in fifteen minutes.' My heart pounded. Soon we would be boarding a bus into Pittsburgh.

"At the auditorium an usher led me to a seat in back. I eased myself into it, settling Patrick with me. The place was packed. There were people in wheelchairs jamming the aisles, people on crutches, even on stretchers. I felt lost in an ocean of need.

"Even before the prayer line formed, people were healed, including the man across the aisle from me. I had seen the enormous lump on his neck. But now it was gone. 'Hodgkin's disease,' his wife said, weeping joyously. I'd actually seen a miracle; several, in fact.

But when the service was over, Patrick remained the same.

"Outside, a hot August sun bleached the pavement. Dead tired, I boarded a bus back to the airport. Disappointment smothered me. I felt as if God were gone from my world. By the time I carried Patrick to the plane and got seated, I was feeling nauseated. If I didn't sleep I would collapse. A middle-aged man in a pin-striped suit sat next to me. Sliding his briefcase under the seat, he glanced over. 'You look so tired. Would you like me to hold your son so you can sleep?'

" 'I would,' I said, 'but he doesn't go to strangers, especially not men.' The man smiled and said he'd give it a try. I held back, explaining about Patrick's condition. 'It's all right,' the man said gently. 'He's God's child too.' I handed Patrick over, bracing for his screams. He truly never let strangers hold him. But my son put his head on the man's shoulder and drowsed.

"I fell into a deep sleep immediately, awakening only as we were landing. The words 'God's child' were on my mind. My nausea was gone. I felt refreshed. Patrick was still sleeping. The man insisted on carrying him off the plane and back to my car. As I fastened Patrick in his car seat, I thanked the man and said I was all right now. Still he wouldn't leave.

" 'I'll just wait until you get your car started,' he said.

" 'You've done too much already.'

But he insisted. I got in the car and turned the key in the ignition. The battery was dead. In my eagerness that morning, I had left the headlights on.

" 'Don't worry,' my benefactor said. 'I'm parked in the next lot. Just wait here and I'll get your car started.' He was soon back with jumper cables, charging the battery. I tried to pay him, but he wouldn't hear of it. 'God sent me to you,' he said.

"As I threaded my way home through the traffic, I glanced in the rear view mirror at Patrick. His head was flopped over in sleep, chocolate cookie crumbs around his mouth. The leaves on trees flanking the highway looked black against the dusky pink sky. The last of the sun filtered through puffy gray clouds. The day was nearly done, a chapter closed.

"I had gone to a service so Patrick could be healed. When I turned into our driveway, and saw Whitney at the door, I knew I'd traveled a road to acceptance. And that was the miracle God had waiting for me." [20]

Prayer will help you keep the balance through the agonies and the ecstacies of life. After the famous Los Angles earthquake a woman on television was thanking the Lord. She had lost everything, but she still had the Lord and was so thankful, while others were thinking of the destroyed possessions. The contrast was so stark between the depressed people interviewed and this praising woman.

Prayer can calm us even in the midst of great tragedies. We must pray so frequently that it is habitual. How many of us forget to pray when we encounter a problem until we finally realize we can't solve it. We should call on Jesus immediately. Jesus is the Eternal Angel who comes before we call. "...Teacher, do you not care that we are perishing? He woke up, rebuked the wind, and said to the sea, 'Quiet! Be still !' ". The wind ceased and there was great calm. Then He asked them, "Why are you terrified? Do you not yet have faith?" (Mark. 4:38-40, NAB)

Hurricane Andrew demolished a section of South Miami and people were fortunate to escape with their lives. What some people had worked all their lives for was gone in a short time. What an emotional jolt. Only Jesus can carry people through that trauma. Scripture tells us here we have no lasting home. Without a strong prayer life there is the tendency to think that this is the end of all life. We must stay in touch with the eternal by serious prayer. This is important for good mental and emotional health.

I once asked people where north was. The people pointed in all directions. Most were wrong. With a compass I pointed out north. In the same way, our prayer points us like the compass to the eternal happiness of Heaven where we shall live forever with our relatives and friends.

So many lives are being destroyed by divorce

these days. It is questionable whether a person ever really gets over the hurt and pain of this phenomenon. However, prayer has helped many stabilize their life. I recall giving a retreat and a woman had received divorce papers from her husband with whom she expected reconciliation. She was in a daze on retreat, especially the first night, because her husband had asked for a divorce. She participated in all the prayer exercises as best she could under the circumstances. At the end of our retreat, she was a new person transformed by a special touch of God's grace. It was hard to believe what I saw and heard. She was smiling and witnessed how she experienced God's love and presence. This was one of the most dramatic changes I have ever witnessed. God worked through the time of prayer.

"I love the Lord, who listened to my voice in supplication, Who turned an ear to me on the day I called... Then I called on the name of the Lord, 'O' Lord, save my life' " (Psalm 116: 1-2 & 4, NAB).

How often have I heard a parent say, "When my child died I almost lost my mind, but my prayer life kept me sane." Some of life's hurts are almost impossible to endure. Some do "snap" and kill themselves rather than continue in the pain.

Psychologists list death as the greatest trauma. Frequently people come to a healing service because they cannot get over the death of a loved one. Many are healed. The others have to continue their daily prayer asking for healing.

Two men in their forties were ordained to the

priesthood in the Boston Archdiocese. Both of them stated that they had seen their fathers die of cancer and were struck with how frail human life is, and decided to become priests. They did not know each other when they made their decisions. Both were ordained at the same time.

Loss of reputation is also a tremendous pain. The following story illustrates this:

Donna Rice Finds Healing After Scandal

After losing her reputation in a political sex scandal, the former model had returned to the faith of her childhood.

"Eight years ago, Donna Rice made headlines as the woman who toppled Colorado senator Gary Hart's bid for the presidency. She was caught by reporters emerging with Hart from his Washington, D.C., townhouse, and it soon was discovered that she also had accompanied the married politician on a private pleasure cruise to the Bahamas. The yacht's name -- Monkey Business -- seemed appropriate.

Except for an interview with Barbara Walters, Rice never spoke publicly about the scandal and soon dropped out of sight.

Today, Donna Rice-Hughes is happily married, and she's a committed Christian. She's also making headlines again, this time because of her work with Enough Is Enough!, an anti-pornography organization. Currently, the group is lobbying Congress to pass legislation that would ban illegal pornography from the Internet and other computer services.

" 'Isn't this just God's sense of humor to have me speaking out on an issue dealing with sex?' " Rice-Hughes asked *Charisma.* She is quick to confirm, however, that her journey from political scandal to pro-family crusade was no laughing matter.

"She grew up in a Christian home in Columbia, S.C., where she accepted Jesus in the ninth grade at First Baptist Church. After graduating from the University of South Carolina, she entered and won the Miss South Carolina World Pageant. That landed her in New York, where she pursued a modeling and acting career.

"Now 37, Rice-Hughes says it was a series of subtle compromises in her 20s that led her to the 'fast track' of the 1980s and away from her faith. 'I reluctantly betrayed my own conscience, and I knew better,' she said.

"Although she was with Hart on only two occasions, the ensuing media scandal changed her life forever. The resulting pressure forced her to resign from the Miami pharmaceutical firm where she worked as a sales representative, and she abruptly lost her work in TV commercials.

"Close friends and associates sold photos of her, along with their version of her story. And her family stood by humiliated as she was portrayed as a prostitute or worse.

"At a spiritual crossroads in her life, Rice-Hughes says she ultimately had to decide whether to place her trust in the Lord or in a bank account. The media lured her down one path with offers totaling more than $5 million if she would sell her story for a book or a TV movie-of-the-week.

" 'Had I gained fame through an achievement, that would have been different,' she said. 'But I became notorious because of a mistake for which I was very much ashamed. So I could not allow myself to exploit the opportunities.'

"The media feeding frenzy intensified as the 1988 presidential race heated up. Rice-Hughes felt like shark bait. By that point, God had gotten her attention.

" 'God let me fall on my rear end in front of the whole world and lose everything that was my identity -- my reputation, my ability, my achievements,' she said. 'Here I was, a Phi Beta Kappa, but now I was known as a bimbo.'

"Her prayer was that God would pick up the pieces and make something good from her life. He began to answer

that prayer almost immediately.

" 'All of a sudden, God's people kept surrounding me and helping me make decisions during this devastating, dark time,' she explained.

"The epitome of that support came when some Christians invited her to The Cedars, a sequestered retreat in northern Virginia. She stayed there for three months, then moved in with a Christian family and spent the next several years in isolation and quiet solitude.

"Her journey back to the Lord, Rice-Hughes said, was one of 'baby steps' while she worked through her anger, depression and post-traumatic shock. Women's Bible studies and support groups were an important part of her recovery. True peace finally came when she stopped worrying about restoring her reputation.

" 'Reputation is who others think you are; character is who you really are,' she explains. 'I believe that a mark of someone's character is not in the mistakes they make but in how they choose to handle them. I discovered that how I lived my life after the scandal would say more about me in the long run.' " [21]

Not only pain, but even success can derail our relationship with God. How many movie stars speak about their relationship with Jesus? Some like Pat Boone do. Many, however, seem to have adopted a pagan lifestyle. A strong prayer life can keep success from going to one's head. It can keep us from changing in the wrong way. We must always keep the bottom line in mind. "...For you are dirt, and to dirt you shall return" (Genesis. 3:19, NAB).

When a new pope is elected, there is the burning of flax and the chaplain cries out: "Thus passes the glory of this world." In this way the new Pope is shown how frail and passing one's life is, and he is exhorted to follow Jesus whole-heartedly. Some of the old monks kept a human dried up skull on their desk to remind them that death was coming to them someday.

Prayer energizes the Christian. Reading the lives of the saints, I noticed that many of them slept very little. It was clear that they were energized by prayer. This was a time of great peace and fulfillment, and they received more than if they had been sleeping.

"Come to me, all you who labor and are burdened, and I will give you rest" (Matthew 11:28, NAB).

People who make occasional all-night vigils tell me that they are elated by the night of prayer and merely shower when they go home. They peacefully go to work, filled with enthusiasm.

One night I was having a deep sense of Our Lady's presence and I found it quite easy to pray. The night passed quickly and dawn came before I realized it. This was the shortest night of my life. Yes, I had energy to burn during the day.

A friend was directed by a doctor to meditate 20 minutes in the morning and 20 minutes in the evening to reduce stress. Most of us have experienced a deep peace as we finished our prayer.

Meditation has found its way into Wall Street in New York, according to an article in the USA TODAY. Edward Bednar teaches business people how to pray and get that deep relaxation that will make them more efficient in their work.

"His meditation classes are one of many paths that workers are exploring as more of them try to combine their spiritual values with their work life. 'The cumulative corporate hurt' employees feel over downsizing and the disappearance of job security is forcing people to look at work differently, says Phyllis Tickle, religious books editor at Publishers Weekly. Books with a religious bent are one of the fastest-growing segments -- showing a 45% sales increase in March over the previous year. Tickle says books combining spiritual themes and business issues are fueling that growth. Books such as *Jesus CEO; A Higher Standard of Leadership; Lessons from the Life of Gandhi; The Soul of a Business;* and *Thunder in the Sky,* based on an ancient Chinese text, all have proven surprise sellers.

"But it doesn't surprise Bednar. 'I don't see an adversarial role between the contemplative view of the world -- which values community and personal relationships -- and the bureaucratic, goal-oriented, financially viable corporate world,' he says. 'I believe the two can be integrated.'

"So do many others.

"In Chicago, a group of Catholic professionals formed The First Friday Club so that they 'could take an hour out of the workday once a month and hear people talk about how you can connect your value system and faith life with what you do every day,' says Bill Yacullo, an executive search consultant and one of the group's founders.

"At the Ford Motor plant in Hazelwood, Mo., a non-denominational prayer group meets regularly. Lotus Development has formed a 'soul committee' to examine the company's value system.

"The trend has spawned new businesses. From a few dozen customers 10 years ago, Sounds True Audio, a Colorado mail-order audio tape company, now reaches a subscriber list of 130,000 in North America and Europe with its tapes on spirituality, meditation and personal development." [22]

"Rising very early before dawn, he left and went off to a deserted place where he prayed (Mark 1:35, NAB). Jesus was energized by this communication with His Father. Are we not uplifted by good fellowship with a friend or member of our family? How much more should we be elevated by our conversation with the Lord Jesus and His heavenly Father?

Communication gives rise to love, so our whole life is improved by our interaction with Jesus in prayer. We can unburden ourselves to Him and be inspired and encouraged by him. But it is most helpful if we already believe that Jesus will help us.

The following is an interesting story about a minister who was looking for a word that meant "believe":

One Weighty Word

"In the 19th century, missionary John Paton journeyed to the New Hebrides Islands in the southwestern Pacific, where he began to translate Scripture into the inhabitants' native tongue. Discovering that there was no equivalent for the word believe, he tried to find a term or phrase to convey the meaning of the word.

"One day a worker came into his office, worn out from a hard day's physical labor. The man collapsed into a chair. Then he stretched out and rested his legs on another chair. He told Paton it felt good to lean his whole weight on those chairs. Immediately Paton noted the expression the man used for 'lean my whole weight on.' He knew he had found the right term for the English word believe" (John Parachin, Virginia Beach, Virginia).[23]

Many will agree that prayer does energize and help a weary Christian relax and live in a deeper peace, but they do not have or take the time for it.

Teaching in Santiago, Chile, some years ago, I suggested that people start with five minutes a day of prayer, and every week add five minutes. Years later, revisiting the city, a man told me that he now prayed three hours a day using that method.

A woman who had a retarded son was blamed by her jealous husband for giving all the attention to the boy. She was in a real bind. Yelling out at the Lord, she felt Him saying, "Make a holy hour daily." After doing this, her problem dissolved. Later she said: "There is little that will not be healed by an hour of prayer a day." What peace and relaxation one experiences in that time.

Many parents are worried about their children and grandchildren. They need to pray them into Heaven. Daily, these older and wiser parents need to spend serious time asking the Lord to touch and heal their family. The grace of conversion will come through the prayers of the parents. They have an obligation to pray their family into Eternal Life. Conversion of some sort will come, but frequently it's after the parents die.

Jesus invites us to ask for whatever we need. That covers the spectrum from spiritual needs such as conversion for a family member, psychological and emotional needs, relationships, and even bodily wholeness. It will change us, and change our lives.

Retired people who have invested their time in daily prayer find deep fulfillment in their older age. One can feel the spiritual energy and joy in these "wise and prudent servants". May I be more like them.

Lord, give me the energy of the saints who had incredible energy to do your work. As I pray during the day, empower me to go joyfully and peacefully through the day. What You have done for so many, You want to do for me. Let me be open to Your miracles of grace through deep faith, trust and love. Walk with me as I walk the path of life. Help me know there must be the good and bad, sweet and sad. With you holding my hand, guide and direct me every minute of my life. Amen.

Chapter VI

God Always Answers Prayer In Some Way

The Lord in reply said to her: "…Martha, Martha, you are worried and bothered about so many things; but only a few things are necessary, really only one, for Mary has chosen the good part, which shall not be taken away from her." (Luke 10:41-42, NAB).

Mary "shall not be deprived of it". She chose to listen to Christ, and thus became a great person of prayer. In this scripture, some scholars speak of a different translation. They say the translation could be: "Only one dish is necessary" rather than "Only one thing is required". Jesus was satisfied with a simple meal. Martha could have joined Mary in listening to Jesus, had she kept it simple. Mary was rapt in absorbing what Jesus was saying. She was in a receptive frame of mind, and was being nourished spiritually by the words of Jesus. But her sister Martha worked excessively at cooking the meal, and her overzealous work in preparing physical food was substantially inferior to the spiritual food given to Mary.

Some time later, God quickly answered the prayers of all three Marys who most intensely wanted to see the risen Christ. Mary Magdalene, Martha's sister Mary, and the Blessed Virgin Mary were the first to see Jesus in his glorified body. Though formerly a great sinner, Mary Magdalene was converted personally by Jesus and subsequently was the first one to go to the empty tomb, and the very first person on earth to see the risen Christ. Mary Magdalene went to the disciples: " ... 'I have seen the Lord' ...," (John. 20:18 NAB) she announced. Then she reported what He had said to her, that He had not yet gone up to the Father but that He was going up to His Father and her Father. Shouldn't Mary Magdalene's conversion and great reward give all of us sinners increased hope? She became the first evangelizer announcing the resurrection of Jesus, and *it changed history.*

The Lord wants to love us and guide us into the way of happiness and peace. When we go into prayer, we open ourselves to be touched, blessed, and guided by the Holy Spirit. In prayer, we open ourselves to the presence of Jesus. When we do, we are tuned in to Him. When our television set is not tuned in perfectly, we get a blurred picture and most of us will not stand for that. We want a perfect picture. Sometimes "we" are not concentrating when we pray and thus we present a "blurred" picture. We can clarify the picture in many ways, for example, through visualization. We can also name the specific persons we are praying for. Sometimes we are "blocked" from praying effectively by unforgiveness or some similar problems. The problem is never with the Lord, it is "always" with us. When we are in deep prayer, the Lord is able to communicate with us better. The Lord is always "most eager" to communicate. When we are in trouble, He comes before we even call:

> **Three principal parables on prayer are transmitted to us by St. Luke: The first, "the importunate friend," invites us to urgent prayer: "Knock, and it will be opened to you." To the one who prays like this, the heavenly Father will "give whatever he needs," and above all the Holy Spirit who contains all gifts...** (The Catholic Catechism #2613).[24]

As a living Father, God always hears and answers prayer, but in His own time and way. In the entire history of our world, there has not been one single prayer that has gone unanswered. Everyone is a winner in prayer, just as virtually all in the lottery are losers. God's response to prayer is an immediate pouring forth of His love. We may never **"see"** the results, because God may want to increase our faith, or test us. On the other hand, we may not see the results until much later, years later, until we die or even after our death. This is because although God's response is immediate, unlike Him, we live in a time ordered world. We see events unfolding in a serial manner. The one thing we can be sure of is that God always blesses us far beyond our merits, and that His infinite blessings are for all eternity.

Jesus said, "If you remain in me and my words remain in you, ask for whatever you want and it will be done for you. By this is my Father glorified, that you bear much fruit and become my disciples" (John 15:7-8, NAB). The term "remain" means to rest in, live in, be absorbed in and to be one with. It is an invitation to absorb the word of God in Scripture, and unite with Him who is the Word of God. This implies (all other things being equal) that our requests will be granted to the extent this oneness exists.

"And I tell you, ask and you will receive; seek and you will find; knock and the door will be opened to you. For everyone who asks, receives; and the one who seeks, finds; and to the one who knocks, the door will be opened" (Luke 11:9-10 NAB).

Prayer to Jesus was always answered by him during his ministry on earth:

Jesus hears the prayer of faith, expressed in words (the leper Jairus, the Canaanite woman, the good thief) or in silence (the bearers of the paralytic, the woman with a hemmorrhage who touches his clothes, the tears and ointment of the sinful woman). The urgent

request of the blind men, "Have mercy on us, Son of David" … Healing infirmities or forgiving sins, Jesus always responds to a prayer offered in faith: "Your faith has made you well; go in peace" (The Catholic Catechism #2616).[25]

What are some of the reasons we don't think God answers prayer today? The primary reason is that we don't see the answer when we expect it, nor do we see it acted upon exactly as we expected. But isn't it rather absurd for us to have such limited expectations of God? We are of low intellect (Lucifer was and remains far more brilliant), in a fog of confusion, and quite unloving. Should we really expect to know in a detailed manner exactly how our infinitely loving, infinitely intelligent God acts and reacts? There is one key thing we know deep down for sure, and maybe that's all we really need to know. God **always responds** to love, He always responds **with love** and, I would dare say with a great deal more eagerness and love and commitment than we do. Not only does God act in love, but He always acts with love towards **all** creatures. Unlike the atheistic bumper sticker that said, "Prayer always fails," PRAYER ALWAYS WORKS in some special way.

If we know God always responds with love, then why do we fear anything? First, because we are so weakened by original sin and by our own sins. It seems to be human nature to be anxious, to worry. Secondly, we haven't built ourselves up spiritually through the sacraments. Thirdly, because we don't pray enough. Because of these things, we do not have a sufficiently intimate relationship with God so that we just automatically call on Him or Mary or Joseph when we need help – we simply don't think to do it. Rather, our first instinct and action is to "fix it *ourselves*".

In daily deep prayer, the Lord also gives us love by affirming us and letting us know how loved we are. He carries us along through the "valleys of darkness." Most experience a life threatening situation at least once in their lives. Some of these could be an experience of deep emotional devastation, like a divorce or the death of a family member. But Jesus wants to walk with us and help us carry our cross. "Come to me, all you who labor and are burdened, and I will give you rest" (Matthew 11:28, NAB).

Joseph Whalen had a high position in AT&T but was plagued by alcoholism. His children avoided him, and his wife was at her wit's end. Finally she divorced him because of the pain he inflicted on everyone. She said to him in the heat of the court battle: "You'll end up in the gutter." Joe became furious. He said: "I feel so rotten about myself that I just don't want to live."

Fortunately, someone directed him to a priest who taught him to say when he felt hatred toward his wife, "God bless Frances." Joe started to pray seriously. Finally he was cured of alcoholism. His marriage was officially annulled by the Boston Marriage Tribunal. He was feeling so much better about himself that he was able to answer the call to the Priesthood. "By the grace of God, I was ordained a Roman Catholic Priest on Sept. 9, 1989, at the tender age of sixty-six by Bishop Alfred Hughes, Auxiliary Bishop of the Archdiocese of Boston, Massachusetts. Isn't it miraculous what God has accomplished in my life . . . There are not enough words in the English language to describe Our Lord's amazing love."

Through prayer, God's grace was able to work a miracle in this down-and-out man to bring him to the altar. Many people have testified how much Father Whalen has helped them. He is an outstanding priest today.

As we give the Lord some minutes out of the 1,440 minutes He gives us each day, the Holy Spirit is able to mold us towards what He wants. All of us will face situations that cannot be changed. Ask through prayer for the grace to accept the unchangeable. Consider the plight of a condemned man who was to be executed in Huntsville, Texas. Through prayer, his fear and terror were healed and he was ready for the inevitable. Joseph Beavers stated to the newspaper reporters, "I believe a man reaps what he sows. I feel I have a debt to pay, a penalty for a crime. It is a hard pill to swallow . . . . I know what to expect. I have no fear of death. I have eternal life. I know I'm going to have a new life." What courage born of prayer and the power of Almighty God!

St. Paul speaks of his difficult times: "But we hold this treasure in earthen vessels, that the surpassing power may be of God and not from us.

108

We are afflicted in every way, but not constrained; perplexed, but not driven to despair; persecuted, but not abandoned; struck down but not destroyed; always carrying about in the body the dying of Jesus, so that the life of Jesus may also be manifested in our body. For we who live are constantly being given up to death for the sake of Jesus, so that the life of Jesus may be manifested in our mortal flesh": (2 Corinthians 4: 7-11, NAB).

The more we trust and love the Lord, the more open we are to all of the blessings He has for us. There was a time when I had always believed only in spiritual healing. Then as I was praying for people after a deep religious experience, I began to see healing of all sorts: physical, emotional, and psychological

Whatever happens, keep praying. Don't give up. "Rejoice in hope, endure in afflictions, persevere in prayer" (Romans 12:12, NAB).

A woman came to me with a terribly sprained wrist and I prayed for healing, and it was instantly made well. I could not believe it. Even though I preached "God answers prayer", I had never seen anything like that, an immediate answer to prayer.

A Vietnam veteran had stayed in his room for one year, coming out only for meals. He would not go to look for a job. His parents were terribly upset. His room was in disarray and dirty. His mother and I prayed one Sunday after Mass that the Lord would touch him and make him well. The next day he went out to look for a job. I could not believe it, nor could his parents. God answered within 24 hours.

Now I have much greater faith and trust in the Lord, as I have seen thousands of immediate answers to prayer. The more I have believed and trusted, the more I have seen the Lord work in my own life.

Two blind men, In Matthew 9, approach Jesus seeking healing. Jesus asks: "…'Do you believe I can do this?' 'Yes, Lord,' they said to him. Then He touched their eyes and said, 'Let it be done for you according to your faith.' And their eyes were opened…" (Matthew 28-30, NAB).

The stronger our spiritual life, the more blessings are ours. Availing ourselves of the sacraments of Penance and Holy Eucharist deepens our faith, trust, and love in a powerful way to enter into deep prayer. Also, the greater our expectation, the more open we are to the work of the Holy Spirit.

The more love we have for the Trinity and people, the more powerful our prayers are. There is rarely a greater love than a mother for her child, and prayers from a mother or father for a child in trouble are most powerful. Our Mother, Mary, is most receptive to these prayers. She is a most powerful intercessor. Love is a gift from God to everybody. We must not destroy it through mortal sin, or even over a period of time through venial sin.

A priest in Africa told me of people walking for a week to get to the neighboring country to visit a bishop who had a healing ministry. They prayed all the way as they made the long journey. He stated that most of them were healed. I won-dered about this. Then it dawned on me that they had great anticipation and openness. It is clear that there are four times as many healings in the third world as in the first world. Frequently, these people have to be healed in the healing service or they will die since there are no medical facilities, nor do they have the money to pay for these services. Obviously they come with great openness.

In the United States, people come in air-conditioned cars and want to park close to the door so they will not have to walk far. Sometimes they complain that it is not cool enough in the church, or the service is too long. You can see the difference between the two groups, the Africans who come at great pain, versus the people in the United States who come at their convenience. Which ones are more open?

Mother Theresa of India is a beautiful example of faith, trust, and love. In ONE HEART FULL OF LOVE [26], she teaches how her faith is able to see Jesus in the poor and dying:

> "The Father loved Jesus and gave him to us. Jesus made himself the Bread of Life, so that we could eat of him and have life. He wants to satisfy our hunger for love and for God.
>
> "As if that were not enough, Jesus became the hungry one, so that you and I could satisfy his hunger, cover his nakedness, and offer him shelter. He said, 'You did it to me. I was hungry. I was naked. I

was homeless.' The forgotten man in the street, the one we picked up in the streets of Calcutta, was Jesus bearing that man's appearance. It was Jesus who was hungry. I will never forget the man who was half-eaten by worms when we found him. He was tenderly carried to the home for those dying destitute. On the way, he murmured: 'I have lived like an animal, but now I am going to die loved and surrounded with care.' That is how he died and went home to God. That was Jesus in the disguise of the poor.

"The poor are great people. The poor deserve love. Do you know the poor in your midst? It would be sad if you didn't know your own poor. Just as love begins at home, so too, poverty begins at home. You need to know who is lonely, unloved, and forgotten in your own homes and communities."

Listen to the Lord in prayer; He will communicate in some way. Our Loving Father, Abba, wants to speak to us and He will do so if we are listening and are hungry for His words. In prayer, we try to listen as much as we can.

"God is love…"(1 John. 4:16, NAB) is the most important scripture in the bible according to some, because it tells us the nature of God. His whole being is pure love. Our job is to be open to receive the love with which He embraces us. The nature of love is to communicate. How many married couples can testify to the time they spent together courting. Sharing ideas, vision, emotions, goals, attitudes brings two people together, so they usually marry.

The Father has said, "...This is my beloved Son,..." (Matthew 3:17, NAB). "For God so loved the world that he gave his only Son,..." (John 3:16, NAB). He speaks to us through His Son.

Jesus again said, "My sheep hear my voice..." (John 10:27, NAB). The powerful part of prayer is the Lord speaking to our heart. He will communicate in multiple ways: scripturally or directly to one's heart, through events, friends, clergy, oftentimes through simple people sharing wisdom, small children, and through many other avenues. He is not limited to one particular way. Generally, He will use all of them.

The big difficulty is that people think they are making up the ideas that are coming into their minds even though they are quite different from what they generally have. One priest who gives prayer seminars around the country, states that what kills the prayer life of most people is that when God speaks through their ideas, they think it is their own ideas and they reject it. We need to trust that the Lord is responding to us at these moments, if it is something positive. It is better to believe too much than too little.

One rule of thumb is to accept any good and different ideas as coming from God, if they edify and make our life more spiritual. If love increases

113

through these ideas, presume they are from the Lord and accept them. Even if they are not, what harm is done if one is built up and affirmed, encouraged and strengthened? One will be better off because of them.

We presume that we are talking to prudent people who will discern these ideas against the scriptures, the teaching of the church, and common sense. A good spiritual director will be of invaluable help in this case. Opportunities often come rather unexpectedly. Consider the following story, which shows how an opportunity for quiet time, for time to reminisce was turned into a wonderful experience with God:

> "Recently my husband went on a two-week hunting trip, and I was alone with lots of time on my hands. For unexplainable reasons I began to dialogue with God. It began with making myself transparent before him insofar as I was able. Almost all my deepest secrets were exposed before Him. I found His acceptance as never before. Later, I discovered His Love. I was also honest about my lack of love for Him and how it pierced my own heart to feel that way. Day after day I went through these confessions, and God spoke to me by use of Scripture. He brought back to my remembrance verses I had read years ago. I had an old King James which had a concordance, so I would look up these

verses. He pointed out to me that I had the Holy Spirit, to 'remain in Him', that I was chosen - predestined even and, most wonderful of all were his words to me: Though you have not seen Him, you love Him and even though you do not see Him now, you believe in Him . . . I didn't know I loved Him -- He had to point it out to me and since then loving Him is getting easier. During those two weeks with the Lord, I ate to survive - was never hungry, got very little sleep -- was never tired and was not the least bit lonely. Jesus was and is the guest of my soul" (Van Varner).[27]

I personally believe most people experience the Lord powerfully at least three times in their life. Once as a child, once as a young adult, and then once as an older person. This conclusion comes from talking with people around the world. Can you recall a time the Lord spoke to you by a strong impression, or a voice in your heart, or even an audible voice? Catholics are often afraid to admit this for fear that people will mock them or deride them. How much we miss by not sharing our experiences.

Listen to this story from my own life:

"Washing my hands after lunch while living in Grenada, West Indies, I heard an audible voice. 'Go to Jamaica'. I looked around and the area was deserted. I knew it was the Lord.

115

"A visitor had asked me to come to Jamaica where she had a teaching center and give some conferences. I declined. She kept asking and I kept resisting. It was only a few days later that the Lord spoke. While I had planned on visiting Jamaica for one week, I ended up spending two full weeks of instructions."

Had God spoken to you? Perhaps we will all be more sensitive to the prompting and articulations of the Lord from now on. The following testimony further illustrates the dialogue that happens with some Christians:

"God and I talk to each other all day long. I'm always asking Him what He wants me to do and He tells me. He tells me to calm down when I'm upset, to trust him when I'm afraid or confused and He's always telling me how much He loves me. He tells me when I've disappointed Him and when I've pleased Him. He calls to me when my mind wanders away from Him. I tell him my concerns. I tell Him how I feel. I complain to Him when things don't go the way I want them to. He listens patiently then tells me what He wants. He consoles me when I'm sad or hurt or lonely. I can feel His arms around me as He holds me close. He sends me into the desert from time to time and I can't feel Him near and He is silent. It's awful! After awhile, He gives me a sign to let me know that I'm not in the desert alone, He is there with me and is watching over me and taking care of me but He wants me to have the faith without the constant consolation. I'm usually a slow learner in that regard. He is so patient with me. When I've learned at least part of the lesson He wanted to teach me, then He gifts me with a wonderful mountaintop experience. His mercy is wonderful. Praise God" (Norman Vincent Peale).[28]

"...With age-old love I have loved you; so I have kept my mercy toward you" (1 Jeremiah 31:3, NAB). From eternity, the Lord has been waiting for us to come to birth so that He could love and nurture us. He waits for us to join Him in eternity to share and fellowship together. Would He not desire to communicate with us in some way? Perhaps it is a dream, a picture in our mind, a book which overwhelms us, a movie, a friend's comments, nature, scripture, a Holy Mass which melts us, or His powerful presence in prayer. Yes, the Lord wants to communicate with you and me. Let us be open.

Lord, I know you love me more than I love myself and want me to be happy. Intellectually, I believe that You always answer prayer. Increase my trust in prayer so that all things will work out for the best. I also pray for the grace of "listening ears" so that I

can hear you better. I want to be more
receptive to Your voice.   Amen

Conclusion

If prayer is to the soul what breathing is to the body, then we must continue talking to the Lord through all the difficulties we will encounter.

Some people inquire, "Is my prayer good?" This is a difficult question since no one is a good judge in his or her own case. If we have a spiritual director, then we can get an objective decision. While most look for a good spiritual director, we have to be content with trusting in the Holy Spirit and read good books on "prayer". Listening to good tapes are helpful, too.

If we are sincerely praying, then there will be an increase in our virtue, for there is immediate interaction between "prayer and virtue" and "virtue and prayer". One strengthens the other.

Therefore, if people tell us that we seem more peaceful, more loving, more trusting, more patient, more compassionate, we can presume that we are praying well.

May this book be a source of encouragement for all the readers and may they continue to "pray always".

FATHER, SEND YOUR BLESSING ON ALL WHO HAVE USED THIS BOOK. GIVE THEM A NEW DESIRE TO SPEND TIME WITH YOU IN PRAYER. SEND THEM AN INSIGHT INTO THE AMAZING POWER OF PRAYER TO CHANGE THEMSELVES, CHANGE THEIR FAMILIES, AND CHANGE THEIR WORKPLACE. COME HOLY SPIRIT, FILL THE HEARTS OF YOUR FAITHFUL AND ENKINDLE IN THEM THE FIRE OF YOUR LOVE. AMEN.

Any young man interested in the work
Of the Josephite Fathers in the African-American community is asked to write to:
Vocation Director
1200 Varnum St., N.E.
Washington, D.C. 20017

References

1. Reprinted with permission from *Associated Press*, 50 Rockefeller Plaza, New York, New York 10030, May 13.

2. Father Robert De Grandis, S.S.J. *The Ten Commandments of Prayer*, HOM Books, 108 Aberdeen St., Lowell, Massachusetts 01825.

3. Libreria Editrice Vaticana. *Catechism of the Catholic Church*, #2744. United States Catholic Conference, 3211 Fourth Street, NE, Washington, D.C. 20017-1194, 1994.

4. *Ibid*, #2565.

5. *Ibid*, #2603.

6. *Ibid*, #2620.

7. Reprinted with permission from *C.N.S.*, 7211 4th Street N.E., Washington, D.C. 20017, April 3, 1996.

8. Source Unknown.

9. Reprinted with permission from *Guideposts* Magazine. Copyright (c)1994 by *Guideposts*, Carmel, New York 10512.

10. Libreria Editrice Vaticana. *Catechism of the Catholic Church*, #2559. United States Catholic Conference, 3211 Fourth Street, NE, Washington, D.C. 20017-1194, 1994.

11. Reprinted with permission from *Guideposts* Magazine. Copyright (c)1995 by *Guideposts*,

Carmel, New York 10512.

12. Reprinted with permission from *Guideposts* Magazine. Copyright (c)1959, 1995 by *Guideposts*, Carmel, New York 10512.

13. Libreria Editrice Vaticana. *Catechism of the Catholic Church*, #2707. United States Catholic Conference, 3211 Fourth Street, NE, Washington, D.C. 20017-1194, 1994.

14. *Ibid*, #2635-6.

15. Reprinted with permission from *Christopher News Notes*, December 1995.

16. Reprinted with permission from *Catholic Digest*, St. Paul, Minnesota, September 1996.

17. Libreria Editrice Vaticana. *Catechism of the Catholic Church,* #2608. United States Catholic Conference, 3211 Fourth Street, NE, Washington, D.C. 20017-1194, 1994.

18. Reprinted with permission from *Guideposts* Magazine. Copyright (c) 1979, 1995 by *Guideposts*, Carmel, New York 10512.

19. Reprinted with permission from *Guideposts* Magazine. Copyright (c) 1995 by *Guideposts*, Carmel, New York 10512.

20. Reprinted with permission from *Guideposts* Magazine. Copyright (c) 1994 by *Guideposts*, Carmel, New York 10512.

21. Reprinted with permission from *Charisma*, Strang Publications, St. Mary, Florida 32746, June 1995.

22. Reprinted with permission from *USA Today*, 1000 Wilson Blvd., Arlington, Virginia 22229,

June 16, 1995.

23. Reprinted with permission from *Guideposts* Magazine. Copyright (c) 1995 by *Guideposts*, Carmel, New York 10512.

24. Libreria Editrice Vaticana. *Catechism of the Catholic Church*, #2613. United States Catholic Conference, 3211 Fourth Street, NE, Washington, D.C. 20017-1194, 1994.

25. *Ibid*, #2616.

26. Mother Theresa, *One Heart Full of Love*, Servant Publications, Ann Arbor, Michigan 48107, 1988.

27. Reprinted with permission from *Guideposts* Magazine. Copyright (c) 1958, 1995 by *Guideposts*, Carmel, New York 10512.

28. Reprinted with permission from *Guideposts* Magazine. Copyright (c)1995 by *Guideposts*, Carmel, New York 10512.

Books By
Father Robert DeGrandis, S.S.J.

The Gift of Miracles $8.00

Healing Through the Mass $8.00

The Word of Knowledge $7.00

Praying for Miracles $7.00

Called to Serve
   (new title for *Come Follow Me*) $7.00

Healing the Broken Heart $6.00

Intergenerational Healing $6.00

Resting in the Spirit $6.00

Renewed by the Holy Spirit $6.00

The Gift of Prophecy $5.00

Layperson's Manual for the
   Healing Ministry $5.00

Growing in Jesus $5.00

To Forgive Is Divine $5.00

Coming to Life $3.00

The Power of Healing Prayer $3.00

The Gift of Tongues $3.00

Inner Healing Through the
   Stations of the Cross $3.00

Forgiveness and Inner Healing $3.00

Self-Image (Healing Life's Emotions) $3.00

Audio Books & Albums by Father Robert DeGrandis, S.S.J

Complete Teaching on the Gifts
  (12 tapes) $40.00
Healing Gifts of the Holy Spirit
  (6 tapes) $26.00
The Gifts of the Holy Spirit
  (6 tapes) $26.00
Maturing in the Gifts (4 tapes) $16.00
God Is Love (4 tapes) $16.00
Set Free (4 tapes) $16.00
Spiritual Gifts (4 tapes) $16.00
Healing of Memories (4 tapes) $16.00
Healing of Ancestors (4 tapes) $16.00
Healing the Family (4 tapes) $16.00
Guidelines for Leaders (4 tapes) $16.00
Healing Through Hearing the Word
  (4 tapes) $16.00
Healing of Self-Image (3 tapes) $12.00
Healing Through the Mass (1 tape) $6.00
Healing Through The Rosary (1 tape) $8.00
Basics of Healing (1 tape) $6.00

Videos
by Father Robert DeGrandis, S.S.J

Gifts of the Holy Spirit (8 tapes).............\$150.00

The Healing Service (5 tapes) \$75.00

Basics of Healing..\$15.00

Healing Through the Mass \$15.00

Gifts of Tongues \$15.00

Jesus Is the Healer \$15.00

Jesus Calls Us to Surrender \$15.00

Jesus Heals Today \$15.00

Jesus Wants to Set You Free \$15.00

We Are in Spiritual Warfare \$15.00

Order from your local bookstore or from:

H.O.M. Books
108 Aberdeen St.
Lowell, MA 01850

Audio Tapes & CDs
"Stories, Songs, & Prayers"
by Fr. Robert De Grandis,
S.S.J. and Cecilia Kittley

Healing Through The Rosary Cassette $9.95
Healing Through The Rosary 2-CD set $19.95
Sing & Pray for Healing (featuring **"The Forgiveness Prayer"**) Cassette $9.95
Sing & Pray for Healing (featuring **"The Forgiveness Prayer"**) CD $14.95
MERCY Cassette- based on **"The Chaplet of The Divine Mercy"** $9.95
MERCY CD-based on **"The Chaplet of The Divine Mercy"** $14.95

Log on to **www.degrandisssj.com** to hear samples and order CDs & tapes,

or write to

Fr. DeGrandis/Cecilia
17 Oak Harbor Drive
Houston, Texas 77062
U.S.A.